GREAT
EXPLORERS

GREAT
EXPLORERS

WHSMITH

EXCLUSIVE
· BOOKS ·

Executive Managers:	Kelly Flynn
	Susan Egerton-Jones
Editor:	Avril Price-Budgen
Art Editor:	Sue Hall
Researchers:	Pamela Mayo Dale
	Winifred Walker
Picture Research:	Millicent Trowbridge
Production:	Peter Phillips

This edition produced exclusively
for W H Smith

Edited and designed by the
Artists House Division of
Mitchell Beazley International Ltd.
Artists House
14–15 Manette Street
London W1V 5LB

"An Artists House Book"
© Mitchell Beazley Publishers 1988

ISBN 0 86134 113 9

Typeset by Hourds Typographica, Stafford.
Reproduction by La Cromolito s.n.c., Milan.
Printed in Portugal by Printer Industria Grafica Lda.

CONTENTS

*M*en and women have been excited by the adventure of exploration ever since man first ventured from his home valley into the next and encountered people and places different to his own. The challenge of venturing into the unknown has been hard to resist even when it has meant putting lives at risk.

The mere mention of space travel today conjures up for us the vast spaces and great distances between the stars and planets but for the early sailors the crossing of unknown oceans and landing in unfamiliar continents was just as great a step for mankind as Armstrong's first step on the moon. Indeed they faced many similar dangers and fears, the only difference today being the wealth of technology backing most ventures and pushing man further and further into the unknown.

We owe much to the first intrepid explorers such as Marco Polo and Columbus who risked their lives in dedicated efforts to discover and cross new continents and who, over the centuries, made navigation and chart and map making into a science. Without them the exploits in more modern times of such as Alcock and Brown, Sir Francis Chichester and Yuri Gagarin to name but four, would not have been possible.

(Left) This Phoenician silver bowl, decorated with gilt, shows combat between warriors, lions and sphinxes.
(Below) The Phoenicians had mastered the art of using glass for decoration. These glass beads were used as pendants.

What we know about the Phoenicians has been assembled from writings in the Bible, Assyrian royal records and classical writers of the past, but we have no continuous account of their history and it has had to be patched together to form a picture.

We use the term Phoenicians collectively but there was no one Phoenician kingdom. The name was given by the Greeks to the city-states along the strip of coast on the eastern shore of the Mediterranean, where Lebanon is now. When this area was invaded from the east these city-states looked to the sea for their livelihood and became the greatest of sailors and sea traders, learning and profiting from their contacts with other Mediterranean countries. Their temples and inscriptions were in the Egyptian style, their architecture showed contact with Mycenae in Greece, and their silver had a Cretan influence, and so on.

It seems strange that they left no records as they were the people who gave us the alphabet which you are reading now. There were probably two alphabets which developed at a similar time. One was lost when Ugarit, one of the city-states, was destroyed in the 13th Century BC, but the other was adopted by the Greeks from whom we have inherited it.

These city-states – Tyre, Sidon, Byblos and Ugarit – were known about as far back as the 14th Century BC. An Egyptian school exercise at that time asked "What is Uzu (the land city of Tyre) like? They say another town is in the sea, named Tyre-the-Port. Water is taken (to) it by the boats and it is richer in fish than sand". This is a reference to the island-city of Tyre. During their history the Phoenicians came under the domination and influence of other countries such as Assyria, the Babylonians, the Persians and the Greeks. Under the Persians they were well-treated and while they paid regular taxes they could trade as they wished. They built ships for Persian attacks against Greece and were very prosperous. A hundred ships were recorded at

This wall relief in a palace at Khorsabad, Iraq, shows the type of boat (hippi) used on the rivers.

anchor in Sidon in the 4th Century BC and the Tyre controlled much of the surrounding coast.

The Building of the Great Mole

Then at about this time Alexander the Great captured Sidon and Byblos. Tyre refused to be captured and for seven months Alexander laid siege to the island-city. His engineers built a "great mole" from the mainland to the island and his army eventually stormed Tyre and took it. That original mole is the basis for the piece of land that even today connects Tyre to the mainland.

This was not the only time that Tyre had been besieged. The Babylonians, under Nebuchadnezzar, had besieged the city for 13 years (from c.585–572 BC), but Tyre had been able to with-

stand so long because the people had been able to get food and stores from the sea throughout the siege. A description from this time describes the various products which had been imported – "fir trees from Amanus, cedars from Lebanon, oak from Bashan, linen from Egypt and seamen from many sources".

Not much is known of the government of each city but they did have a King and Queen who acted as chief priest and high priestess. There was a council of elders which were at times subject to the domination of rulers such as the Assyrians.

Each city had its own Gods which changed at different times, but they all seem to have had a supreme male god, his wife who had many children, and a young male god who was reborn each year with the passage of the seasons.

They were certainly great traders, but they were also fine craftsmen. As well as their skills as silversmiths, weavers, carpenters and masons – they helped to build King Solomon's temple in Jerusalem – they made a famous and very expensive dye from murex shell which gave a range of colours in pinks and purples.

Over and above this they were bold and brave sailors and explorers who were the first people from the civilized world to go beyond the "Pillars of Hercules" – the Straits of Gibraltar – to look for their minerals and other trading goods. They have left signs of their visits on the west coast of Brittany and the Cornish coast and may even have reached Ireland. It is also possible that they rounded the southern tip of Africa and may even have sailed right round the continent.

Before they learned to build walls under water, the Phoenician harbours were cut out of rocks to form a quay which would give shelter against the weather. The rock may have been built up on the weather side. The main harbours were on inhabited islands, and ships unloaded their cargo onto small boats if they anchored away from shore.

They were master sailors who taught the Greeks a new way of guiding ships by the stars so they must have been able to sail at night, and they were also master shipbuilders.

They were most famous for their warships which the Persians were to use in their seafights against the Greeks. The warships had a ram in the front, a merchant ship's bows were rounded. Both had a sail and a mast which could be lowered, both had upper decks and both were rowed by two banks of oars on each side. These would be called biremes. The trireme had three banks of oars and the wide Phoenician hull unlike the narrower Greek one did not need an outrigger. Phoenician galleys were about 120 feet (36 metres) long with 174 rowers in three rows of 29 oars each. The ornaments they carried on board had a religious significance.

Explored the African Coast

In 600 BC Phoenician sailors sent by the Egyptian Pharoah sailed south from the Red Sea to explore the African coast. They would stop at a convenient place on the coast, plant grain, stay there until it was harvested and then sail on further. Whether they did round Africa or not, they had certainly colonized or at least established trading posts and settlements throughout the Mediterranean.

By 800 BC they had built a temple "rectangular in shape and divided up internally with four

(*Above*) This Phoenician statuette of a man with two domestic animals gives us a glimpse of a typical farmer of that time.
(*Left*) Among the items which the Phoenicians used for trading were decorated ostrich eggs for use as bowls.

parallel rows of seven columns" at Kition in Cyprus. Well into the late 8th Century BC the Phoenicians had settled on Rhodes and they were manufacturing and trading perfumed lotions and jewellery. They were decorating their pottery ware and there is evidence that they were producing some of the first glassware. There were also by this time trading posts along the Libyan and Tunisian coasts, in Sicily, Malta and in southwest Spain. Later the Phoenicians traded further along the coast of southern Spain beyond Cadiz and up the Guadalquivir River as far as the mining area of Rio Tinto. We know that their most famous colony, Carthage, was probably founded in 814 BC.

So, for around nine hundred years, until Alexander the Great made them part of the Greek empire, the city-states of Phoenicia had traded and explored and colonized the Mediterranean and though so little of their history is known we have much evidence of the beautiful things they made from the products they collected from the many lands of their exploration.

Although the Phoenicians were great traders their achievements in exploration were no more than was necessary to fulfil the needs of commerce. However, a city closely linked to the Phoenicians, Carthage, was to produce generations of explorers who were to reach as fas as the coast of Britain.

The Carthaginians

The city of Carthage was said to have been founded by the Phoenician princess Dido, who, when she landed on an African shore asked the local chief if she could build a city there. He said that she could build on a piece of land the size of an ox hide, so she had the hide cut up into very tiny strips to cover as large a piece of land as possible. Another story about Dido was that she chose to sacrifice her life rather than marry the

local ruler there.

Neither of these stories is proven and we cannot even say for certain when the city was founded or by whom, but it was most probably settled by Phoenicians from the city state of Tyre in 814 BC. Later, after Nebuchadnezzar, King of Babylon, had subdued Tyre the Phoenicians and Carians fled to the small settlement and it grew to become a large city. This was to be the base for further colonization.

Although Carthage no longer stands, we know that it jutted out from what is the present day Tunis, and that the Carthaginians came to be powerful traders in the Mediterranean Seas.

They were ruthless in their domination and without a qualm would sink the ships of strangers who came into their waters.

They traded with many countries for their imports – they had silver and lead from Spain

Hannibal, whose head appears here on a silver shekel struck at Cartagena c.220 BC, was one of the best known names of the period.

and Sardinia, timber from the Atlas, wheat from Sicily . . . it has been said that they traded the length and breadth of the Mediterranean and beyond and that they had sailed into the Bay of Biscay, had been as far as the River Niger, had travelled across the Sahara Desert and to the English Channel.

Their influence was certainly seen in the western Mediterranean. From inscriptions we know that they had been to Athens, Delos, Thebes and Memphis and imitated the Greeks in such things as clothing and architecture.

We don't really know much about their characters – some writers obviously wrote from hearsay rather than knowledge at the time but they were called "porridge eaters" and it was said they did not drink much alcohol. Plutarch, the great Roman writer, says: "The Carthaginians are hard and gloomy, submissive to their rulers and hard on their subjects, cowardly in fear, cruel in anger, stubborn in decision and austere, caring little for amusement or life's graces." They certainly could not have been cowards or they would not have been such great explorers. Also, since they were known to have had sweet and spiced dishes and to drink wine from fine cups they could not have been too austere.

The people were strong and wiry and wore long clothes. They usually had their heads covered with a kind of fez and headcloth and the men were usually bearded. Their hair was worn straight or curled and kept long with a fringe, or a band to hold it back. They wore expensive jewellery, both men and women wore perfume and people were frequently tatooed. The women seemed to dress like Greeks with robes gathered softly at the waist.

Child Sacrifice

Carthaginian society thought highly of women and most men married only one wife. Children had a largely practical education.

Historians have made much of the awful Carthaginian ritual of child-sacrifice and while they undoubtedly occurred the practice may well have been used only at times of great stress.

For example, in 310 BC Carthage was threatened by invasion, and the Carthaginians thought they had made one of their gods, Kronos, angry.

They had already sacrificed sick children and some who had been "bought for the purpose" to Kronos, but to appease his anger 200 children from noble families were put one by one into the hands of a huge bronze statue of the god and then they were rolled into the fire. The burnt remains from child sacrifices were put into pottery urns and buried.

Besides being traders the Carthaginians were also great explorers. Somewhere probably between 500 BC and 420 BC the Carthaginian Admiral, Hanno, set out on an expedition to look for sea trade around the west African coast, and possibly to set up colonies in the south. Many people believe that he reached Sierra Leone and possibly even the Gulf of Guinea, but it is unlikely that he established regular trade routes. There is no real evidence that they traded further south than Morocco.

The journey to Sierra Leone though, is described in some detail. Hanno was said to have left through the straits of Gibraltar with 60 ships each of 50 oars. He went beyond Sierra Leone, having founded the cities of Mogador and Agadir where he put up temples. He apparently thought, when encountering hostility from local tribes that he had come upon "inhospitable Ethiopians". He saw crocodiles and hippopotami in Senegal and Gambia. He also left an account of an island of wild people whom he described as "hairy". They may have been chimpanzees.

The great seapower of the Carthaginians was to be utterly destroyed when they went to war with Rome over Sicily. They were initially superior to the Romans at sea but the Punic Wars eventually destroyed the Carthaginian "nation" once and for all.

The first, from 264–241 BC, broke their domination of the sea. Then between 218–201 BC the Carthaginians crossed the Alps with Hannibal and his famous elephants, beating the Romans and even threatening Rome. The elephants were, in fact, not altogether a success – they were only seven to eight feet high and could not carry a large amount of equipment. Although they were to provide an element of surprise most of the 27 had died before they reached Italy. Hannibal held out in Southern Italy, but in 204 BC the Romans, under Scipio,

invaded Africa and two years later defeated Hannibal in Tunisia. The Romans went on to defeat Hannibal's brother, Hasdrubal.

The third Punic War from 149–146 BC resulted in a siege which destroyed Carthage completely. The Roman senator Cato's famous words "Delenda est Carthago" – Carthage must be destroyed – were literally put into effect and the city was flattened and even ploughed up. A colony – Colonia Julia Carthago – was later established there by the Romans.

Elephants, shown in the two details of the reverse sides of Carthaginian silver coins, were used regularly as beasts of burden. The Phoenicians' fine metal work was not just restricted to coins as the delicate gold belt shows.

Eric the Red was obviously as hot-tempered as red-haired people are supposed to be, as he appears to have involved himself in feuds wherever he went. This may have been inherited, for his family had left Norway to settle in Iceland around 960AD "because of some killings".

He was banished from Iceland for three years for manslaughter and he left hastily, before the threat to harm his friends and relatives was put into practice. He was literally chased off by his enemies and set sail westward toward the east coast of Greenland. Although there had been sailors' talk of a land far away, he was sailing

The gold, silver and bronze ornaments were very intricately designed, especially the jewellery. The brooches, rings and necklaces were worn by the men as well as the women, the men's jewellery often depicting symbols of their gods particularly Thor the God of War whose symbol was a hammer, seen in the silver pendant here.

into the unknown.

When he reached land he discovered that the fishing was good, parts of the land were fertile, and that livestock could be farmed. There was also an abundance of sea and land animals which could provide furs, hides and tusks.

He survived his exile and returned to Iceland where he soon masterminded an expedition to go back to the land he optimistically called Greenland. Iceland had for years suffered famine and so there was no shortage of volunteers to help him in his venture.

In 985 or 986 about 300 people left Iceland taking with them their livestock and possessions.

Although the voyage should not have taken more than 4 days it proved to be a hazardous, and for some, fatal trip. Only 14 of the 25 ships arrived at their destination. Some sank, others turned back.

Settlements Established

On reaching Greenland, the settlers made their homes in two areas, one under Eric in the southwest, another further north. Although there were some signs that other people had been there, only some stone artefacts and pieces of skin-boats remained.

Eric no doubt enjoyed his rule over the land and in the years that followed more settlers arrived until it is believed there were about 3000 people on 330 farms. Eric had a fine home which even had stream in a stone-lined channel running across its floor, while outside on the green plains grazed his 40 cows.

The Icelanders lived on dairy produce and hunted bears, caribou, whales, seals and fish.

To Leif the Lucky, son of Eric and his wife Thjoohild, is credited the first discovery of North America, although the Icelandic Sagas vary in their accounts. In Eric's Saga, Leif "came upon lands whose existence he had never suspected". But in the Greenland Saga, Leif made a deliberate voyage to find and explore "Vinland".

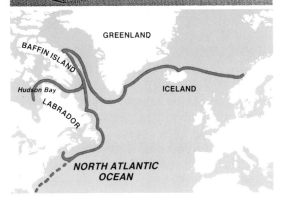

Settlements in Vinland

With a crew of some 35 Leif had apparently landed on Baffin Island, which must have looked very inhospitable with enormous glaciers stretching inland, not a blade of grass to be seen. On his second voyage, however, he first landed in flat, forested country, which sounds like Labrador. He eventually reached the mainland.

The Greenlanders towed their boats up a river, and then they wisely built houses in order to winter over on a lake. These came to be known as Leif's Booths and from these stone and turf shelters they noticed that there was no winter frost. They found that days and nights were more equal in length than at home, and they also discovered the existence of a bounty of wild grapes – hence the name Vinland. Excitedly they sailed back to Greenland with a boatload full (dried by now, we wonder?) as all wine had had to come from the European Continent.

Other Greenlanders returned to Vinland and Leif's Booths were leased to them. The first white child supposed to have been born in North America was the child of Eric the Red's widowed daughter-in-law and her new husband, an Icelander.

Archeological attempts have not yet established exactly where and when the Norsemen did get to, but speculation has variously put Vinland as far afield as Hudson Bay and Florida and many places between.

The Norsemen did not confine their love of decoration to wood and metal as these details of a wall hanging show. They depict Norse gods and goddesses as well as animals of the time.

Marco Polo

(1254–1324)

When Marco Polo and his father and uncle left Venice in 1270, they stayed away on their travels for 25 years. When they returned they had been away so long that no one recognized them, specially as they could no longer speak much Italian! Once they had convinced their close friends and family of who they were, they invited many guests to a spectacular party, appearing in a number of different crimson costumes. Finally they had their old clothes brought in and cut to reveal many beautiful and valuable jewels, so as to prove the wonders they had seen, which Marco Polo later recounted in his book *The Travels of Marco Polo*.

When accused of exaggeration he said he had "not told one half of what I saw". He had crossed Asia and brought back to the west descriptions of China and the countries, with all their spectacle and variety, through which he had passed on his way to get there.

Marco owed his adventures to his father and uncle. As merchants from Venice, then Europe's greatest trading centre, his father and uncle had been persuaded to take the old northern Silk Route to Cambaluc, where Kublai Khan, the mighty Mogul Emperor had his court. There, near what is now Beijing, the Khan helped them in their business and requested the Venetians to ask their Pope to send 100 wise Christians, friars

(Above) Kublai Khan giving his golden seal to the Polos at his new capital, Cambuluc. Having found favour with the Khan, the next 30 years saw the Polos amass riches and honours in China. Situated on the silk route, Cambuluc proved to be the open door for Marco Polo's adventures.

and men "learned in the arts and sciences" to educate "his violent Tartars".

They had been away nine years and Pope Clement VI had died before their return. After the new Pope was elected the brothers put the Khan's request to him, but he appointed only two Dominican friars who, too frightened to continue, returned home soon after setting out with the three Polos – for now the young Marco had joined them.

They decided to travel to China by sea from the Persian Gulf until they saw that the "ships aren't even put together with iron nails but sewn with twine" and chose instead the southern branch of the Silk Route – some 7,000 miles (11,200 kilometres) long. They spent 40 days crossing over the Plain of Pamir reaching 15,600 feet (4,755 metres) before they had then to negotiate the Gobi Desert with its mirages and shifting sands.

Three and a half years after setting out they reached Kublai Khan's court where Marco soon became a favourite, going off on many expeditions in an official capacity and becoming Governor of Yangchow, Imperial Commissioner and Envoy Extraordinary in his 17 years' stay. He saw China's "mighty rivers, its huge cities, its rich manufacture, its swarming population, the inconceivably vast fleets that quickened its seas and its inland waters".

After 17 years working in China the Polos started on their journey home. They took with them the beautiful young princess Cocachin as the new wife for the Khan of Persia. Their voyage as far as Java lasted three months. Once there the crews of their 14 ships built a strong fort to defend themselves against the cannibalistic natives and during their stay there Marco Polo noted the rich variety of spices.

It took two years to reach Persia and of 600 passengers on the 14 ships only 18 survived. The princess was delivered safely. Although the old Khan had died by that time she married Ghazan, his son.

If Marco Polo had not been sent to prison after a sea battle between the Venetians and their trade rivals the Genoese in 1296, shortly after his return, we may not have heard of all the wonders he had seen. A fellow prisoner, Rusticiano, suggested Marco Polo recount to him his long travels – travels which described Hangchow with its 12,000 bridges, Beijing with its 24 miles (38 kilometres) of city walls, eight palaces and a hall large enough to seat 6000 people . . . and countless other wonders.

When Marco Polo came out of prison he lived in Venice for another 25 years in the big family house, parts of which still exist.

(Left) Obviously no pictorial record could be kept by Marco Polo of the sights and events he saw but his vivid description throughout his book allowed artists to depict them later. 1 The Great river Balacian (part of the Oxus). 2 The Sindufu Bridge, Tibet. 3 Indian ships.

1

2

3

Prince Henry the Navigator

(1394–1460)

(Right) Because of their lack of knowledge about the seas beyond their own home waters most sailors believed that they would be attacked by sea monsters such as the one depicted here in an illustration from that period.

Prince Henry is always known as The Navigator. Why was he given this title when he was not even a sailor?

Henry the Infante Dom Henrique was the fourth son of King John I of Portugal. As a Crusader, fighting beside his family in eastern countries to preserve Christianity, he helped to capture the Muslim stronghold at Ceuta, and became a knight. Part of his ambition, then, was to find out if the Moors (a Muslim people inhabiting North West Africa) had a foothold in the unknown lands to the south; to see if there were Christians whom he could press to join him in his fight against the Muslims; and, if there were not Christians, to convert new peoples to Christianity. He was also curious to know what lands lay beyond the Canaries and Cape Bojador, and whether the Portuguese could benefit from trade of such goods as ivory, gold and slaves. Captives could be used as interpreters and for liaison.

Prince Henry started the search for a new route to India. He hoped that he might be able to establish contact with the famed "Prester John", who had already been fighting for the Christian cause, and that together, attacking from two sides, they could finally crush the Muslims. He saw that seapower was the way forward.

Rumours about what lay beyond Cape Bojador were rife: the sea to the south was boiling; white men turned black in the sun! The more real fears of sailing into the unknown were that beyond Bojador, ships with only one mast and sail needed a favourable wind. In addition it was not safe for sailors to land to take on water in hostile Muslim territory.

Azurara, a contemporary historian reported of Bojador that "this much is clear, that beyond this Cape of Bojador there is no race of men, nor place of inhabitants; nor is the land less sandy than the deserts of Libya, where there is no water, no tree, no green herb – and the sea is so shallow that a whole league from land it is only a fathom deep, while the currents are so terrible that no ship, having once passed the Cape, will ever be able to return."

Again and again the patient Henry encouraged his sailors but ships returned time after time without having passed the dreaded Bojador until in 1433 a brave squire went just beyond the Cape and returned with a bunch of flowers from the African coast. Now it was easier for others to show their own bravery and Henry prepared the ships well and made conscientious plans for each expedition.

The Introduction of the Caravel

In 1419 he had established a centre at Sagres where captains could find out the latest accumulation of information. He had charts made of what was known; he brought famous mapmakers, navigators, geographers and ship-

builders together to pool their knowledge and skills and correlate what the returning sailors told them. He made sure that every expedition learned from what had gone before and encouraged the use of navigation instruments such as the mariner's compass, astrolabe, cross-staff, and the mariner's quadrant which helped to determine the line of latitude.

Another important breakthrough was the adaptation of the Portuguese fishing ship, the caravel, which was converted into a ship of some 200 tons and decked with three or four masts.

In 1441 sailors brought back their first gold and slaves and a year later a trading house was set up at Cape Blanco. Once the wealthy merchants realized they could profit from these expeditions they were only too eager to support them and a slave trade grew. What started out as a desire to convert the heathen was now binding people into slavery to the Europeans.

The Portuguese captains ventured further and further south so that by 1446 they had travelled beyond Cape Verde, although they did not land.

By the time Henry died in 1460 his fishermen were trained sailors and navigators; they had reached a wide variety of lands, they had taken the Azores, Madeira and Cape Verde and he had started the journey towards finding a sea route to India and indeed the discovery of America. He has been described as one of the first of the modern colonists.

Many future sailors were able to build on the careful foundations laid by Henry. Bartholomew Diaz, for example, sailed around Africa in 1488, showing that the ocean route to India was obviously possible and that the knowledge now gained was ready to be used in future expeditions.

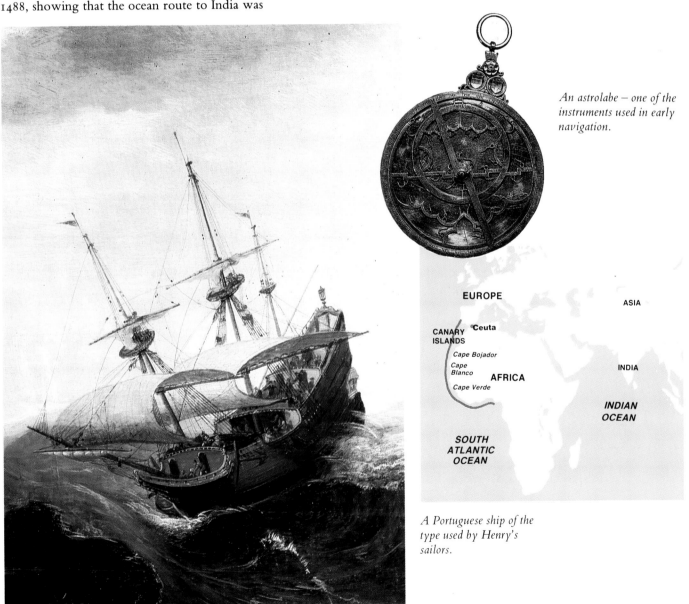

An astrolabe – one of the instruments used in early navigation.

EUROPE

ASIA

CANARY ISLANDS

Ceuta

Cape Bojador

Cape Blanco

AFRICA

INDIA

Cape Verde

INDIAN OCEAN

SOUTH ATLANTIC OCEAN

A Portuguese ship of the type used by Henry's sailors.

reach the Spice Islands and Japan by sailing a voyage of some 2500 miles (4000 kilometres).

Columbus had done some trading in the Mediterranean, had visited the Guinea coast of Africa and, though he was a trader more than a seaman, he also felt he had a mission. He was religious man with a firm faith in God and his own destiny, and he was motivated partly by a desire to find people to convert to Christianity.

First he tried to interest the Portuguese king in his proposals. Then he tried the Spanish Queen Isabella, but she was intent on conquering the last Moorish stronghold in Spain. It was not until after the Moors were finally conquered in 1492 and thanks to the influence of Isabella's treasurer, the Queen agreed to grant Columbus the title of hereditary viceroy of all lands he discovered and a tenth of all value in trade and he was given command of three small ships – the *Santa Maria,* the *Nina* and the *Pinta*. He left in August 1492, now about 40 years old.

He and his men would sail 12,000 miles (19,200 kilometres), not the 2,500 miles (4,000 kilometres) they thought. Navigation was imprecise – they could only guess at longitude. By the time they had been 33 days without seeing land the crew were mutinous. However, land was sighted early on the morning of 12 October 1492.

Columbus and his crew were pleased to find that the inhabitants were very friendly and wore gold nose rings, but they were rather a primitive people with crude homes who lived on plants and the animals about them. Where were the large cities and the rich cloths and jewels? However, they had found land, gold and new people to convert to Christianity.

Still in search of Cathay they travelled on to Cuba, and then to a land of "many harbours on the coast of the seas and many rivers good and large" with high islands and mountains. Columbus named it Hispaniola and again found the Arawak Indians to be "guileless and generous with all they possess" even though there was evidence of cannibalism. Columbus hurried back with the news of what they had found. The King and Queen were treated to a fine display of gold, flowers, fruit, stuffed and live birds, even some Indians from the West Indies, as they were named.

Far from discovering a sea route to the Spice Islands, as he had hoped, Christopher Columbus discovered a new world, and opened the way for the exploration of the Americas.

An age of exploration followed the accomplishments of Prince Henry The Navigator (see page 18), and Columbus, although Italian by birth came under the influence of Portuguese explorers after he settled in Lisbon. He had married ·the daughter of a sea-captain who had served Prince Henry, and he learned such skills as how to handle a caravel and what stores and trading goods were needed on lengthy voyages.

At that time, while it was realized that the earth was a sphere (although Columbus believed it was pear-shaped and that the sea would rise as he sailed westwards) it was thought to have a circumference about one third less than we know it to be. Marco Polo had thought also that Asia was much broader (see page 16), and sharing this belief, Columbus thought he could

De Infulis nuper in mari Indico repertis

Columbus was convinced he had been near Japan and that he would find the Asian mainland and set off again in 1493, this time in grand style with 17 ships and at least 1200 men to colonize Hispaniola.

On his second arrival he discovered that the garrison that he had left had been murdered by natives from another island. The sea was named Caribbean after the savage Caribs. A settlement was made but the settlers, in an unhealthy spot, and because they were short of their western food all treated the natives very badly. There were no spices except for pepper, and gold could only be obtained by slave labour. Columbus was asked to return from his failed mission. He did make two more voyages – on one discovering the mainland of South America, but his weak

yet ruthless rule resulted in his being returned to Spain "in chains" after it was learned that Indians were being enslaved and settlers being hanged.

He was allowed one later voyage on condition he go nowhere near Hispaniola. When he finally returned to Spain in 1504 he was still convinced the Spice Islands were within easy reach. He never realized the full importance of his discoveries. Why had he not listened when on his fourth voyage the Mayan Indians had told him of riches further inland?

(Left) Columbus landing in Hispaniola. These details depict the ships of the time and are taken from one of the first contemporary pamphlets printed at Basle in 1494.

John & Sebastian Cabot
(John died 1498, Sebastian 1483–1557)

Much of the exploration of the Cabots is lost in the past – indeed such conflicting reports of John Cabot's second voyage have one account ending with his complete disappearance along with four of his ships, while another has him returning without spice but with his own cargo almost intact.

Little is known of his early years, but what is certain is that England and John Cabot were useful to each other at a time when Mediterranean merchants were still searching for trade routes westwards to the Spice Islands and the English were not yet making any attempts to sail the Atlantic.

Although there were trained seamen sailing out of the English trading ports, the "island of Brazil" which was supposed to lie near the west coast of Ireland had not been reached, so that

when the Genoese spice merchant came to England some time toward the latter end of the 15th Century he received far more encouragement from Henry VII than he had from the Spanish king. He had a knowledge of geography and was a good navigator and had experience of trading in Mecca. He had asked the King of Spain for the same sort of support he had given Columbus (see page 20), but to no avail.

England was paying high prices for its spices and so Henry gave Cabot permission to sail under the English flag "to all parts, regions and coasts of the eastern, western and northern sea", "to find lands not yet known to Christians to take them in the name of the King". While Henry did not wish to anger Spain, he did not like the idea of Spain and Portugal alone dividing the lands west of the Atlantic among

*(**Right**) Sebastian Cabot.*

themselves.

Cabot set off in the *Matthew* in May 1497 and landed at Newfoundland and Nova Scotia thinking he had come to "the country of the Grand Khan". A letter from the period describes the sea as "swarming with fish, which can be taken not only with the net, but in baskets let down with a stone. I have heard the Messer Zoane Caboto state so much." These would be the Newfoundland Banks, reached after 54 days sailing. Cabot realized though that Marco Polo's (see page 16) descriptions did not fit this primitive land, and thought he had landed north of the civilized areas and raised the flags of England and St Mark of Venice at what was most probably Cape Degrat.

Sailing southwest along the coast he found evidence of habitation but as they were running short of supplies they did not stop. They had an easy journey home, returning to Bristol in August 1497, before going on to London by horse to give an account to the King.

"Genial and Cheerful Liar"

He was rewarded with £10 from Henry which he apparently spent partly on "gay apparel". Almost exactly a year after his first expedition he set out again with five ships still hoping to find the Spice Islands. Some historians believe he reached the American coast and sailed southwards, and to conform to his brief only to discover lands in a similar latitude to England, he drew his coast line east and west rather than northeast and southwest. Other historians claimed that one ship turned back and the others, with Cabot aboard, were lost forever. One source claims that he was on the ship which returned, and died at home.

After John Cabot died, Sebastian continued his father's tradition but as he has been described as a "genial and cheerful liar", it is hard to know whether his ultimate reputation as a famed mapmaker and navigator was warranted.

By the time he left in 1508 or 1509 to seek a northwest passage to Asia, it was known that America was now a new continent. He sailed as far as the Hudson Bay, seeing "numerous masses of ice" even in mid-July, and the daylight lasted for almost 24 hours out of 24. He returned after sailing as far as Chesapeake Bay leaving the way

open for the eventual British claim to North America. He sailed for a while under the Spanish king, but lost favour after a failed attempt to find the South West Passage via the la Plata Valley.

After returning to England he governed a "Company of Merchant Adventurers for the Discovery of Regions Unknown" and was the inspiration for later attempts to find a North East Passage which led to trade between England and Russia.

On his death bed he was reported to have said that he had acquired the "knowledge of the longitude . . . by divine revelation".

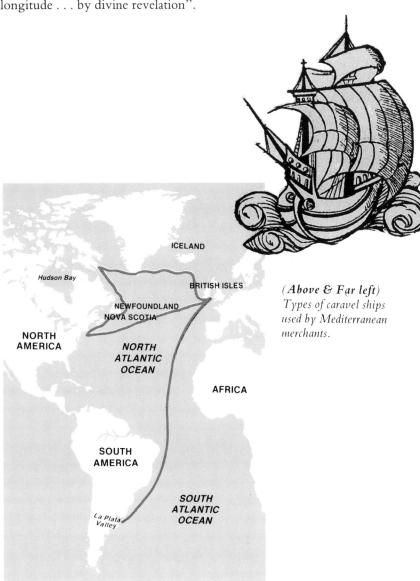

(Above & Far left) Types of caravel ships used by Mediterranean merchants.

Vasco da Gama

(1460–1524)

When Vasco da Gama set sail for India he took with him 18 condemned criminals. They were to be used to try to make friends with new peoples the expedition encountered, and if they survived they were to be pardoned. Whether they did or not we do not know, but it is unlikely as about half the passengers on the expedition did not return.

What we do know is that Vasco da Gama, chosen partly for his firmness and ruthlessness, alienated many people just because of these qualities and his cruelty, even for those days, made him and his people much hated in many of the places he reached.

For nearly 70 years the Portuguese had been working toward the sea voyage to India and great plans were made, including the building of new ships (two of them constructed by Bartholomew Diaz) (see page 19). Goods were loaded on for trading and also to use as presents. They did not know either that their gifts would prove unworthy in the face of the much greater wealth they would encounter.

Vasco da Gama was probably born in the year Henry the Navigator died (1460) into a noble family in a small Portuguese port. He worked on fleets and in "maritime affairs", picking up knowledge of navigation and mathematics that would lead to his selection as Captain Major of the expedition of 1497.

Four ships set out in mid-July with da Gama in charge of the Sao Gabriel and his brother leading her sister ship the Sao Rafael. There were between 140 and 170 men aboard.

Instead of staying close to the coast where he would have the Doldrums and the Guinea current to contend with, da Gama, with typical daring and skill sailed out into the Atlantic from the Cape Verde islands. They were out of sight of land for three months, a lot longer than Columbus's 33 days (see page 20).

When da Gama sailed back to the African coast he landed at Santa Helena, just above Cape Town, where the initial friendly contact with some Hottentots changed to belligerence and the Captain Major was slightly wounded.

Again, after he landed at Mossel Bay, where Diaz had been before him, he encountered hostility from local people. Despite this they remained almost two weeks while they broke up their store-ship and transferred its contents to their other ships.

Now da Gama crept up the east coast of Africa stopping at various places. He gave Natal in the southeast its name when he landed there on Christmas Day. He was encouraged to travel further northwards to name the land he discovered the "Land of the Good People", because of the friendly natives he met near the mouth of the Limpopo.

In Mozambique he came upon four Arab vessels "laden with gold, silver, cloves, pepper, ginger, silver rings . . . . pearls, jewels and rubies." The Sultan disdained the presents he was offered and asked for scarlet cloth which the Portuguese did not have.

While the local Muslims believed their

visitors to be also Muslim they were friendly, but later relations deteriorated, and the cruelty of the Portuguese must have been largely responsible. Again at Mombasa they were not made welcome, which is not surprising when one learns that they tortured two men there with boiling oil until they confessed "that there was a plot afoot to attack the ship". The sailors did however, manage to get some badly needed fresh fruit to help keep down the scurvy which beset them. The cure for scurvy suggested by da Gama was to massage bleeding gums with urine and lance the sores that turned gangrenous.

False Friends

In Mombasa a Hindu pilot was found at the rich and friendly court of the King at Malindi. "The King wore a robe of damask trimmed with green satin and a rich touca". From here the sailors set out for Calicut in India on a trip of 23 days in the false belief that their pilot was Christian. Even when they arrived in India they thought they were in a Christian community and described a temple with "many saints . . . painted on the walls of the church, wearing crowns."

After initially welcoming the travellers the Indians turned on them. This was partly because their gifts were not acceptable (and could hardly have helped Portugal's reputation as country of power), and partly because the Muslims plotted against them. Three months later, having taken some Hindus aboard, da Gama left India, chased out by armed boats.

During the three months' journey back to Africa more men died of scurvy and threats of mutiny were ever present. Once at Mogadishu they had to burn the *Sao Rafael* as she was leaking and they were shorthanded.

Da Gama arrived back in Lisbon in July 1499 two years after he had set out. In some places he had made friends, but he had also made many enemies. What he had done beyond doubt though, was to prove the worth of the Portuguese ships and pave the way for the poor seafaring nation of Portugal to take over the trading supremacy of the Venetians and the Genoese. He had sailed 24,000 nautical miles (44,500 kilometres), and he had returned with a cargo of spices.

Detail of a painting showing Da Gama's ship, Raphael.

Three years later, as Admiral of the Indian Sea, da Gama, commanding ten armed ships, made another trip to India and returned with more spices. He was well rewarded and retired, continuing to act as adviser to the fleets for over twenty years.

In 1524 he was asked to sail again – to try to improve the difficult administration in India. He died on Christmas Eve soon after reaching Cochin. He was in such pain from terrible boils he had that he was unable to speak.

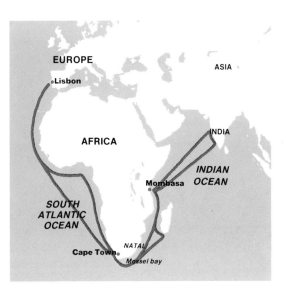

Ferdinand Magellan

(c.1480–1521)

When Ferdinand Magellan set out in 1519 with around 250 men waving their feathered hats from the five brightly painted ships, flags and standards flying, he was not to know that three years would pass and that 40,000 miles (64,000 kilometres) later only one ship would return carrying 18 men – and that he would not be among them.

Magellan had served at the Portuguese court before enlisting to fight for the Portuguese in the East. During the seven years he was twice wounded and as a result was lamed. He fell from grace when he was suspected of being dishonest in connection with the distribution of some booty.

Bitterly hurt, Magellan renounced his Portuguese nationality and joined the Spanish court. If the Portuguese had honoured Magellan as he felt he deserved he would not have had the chance to be granted leadership of the Spanish expedition to find an alternative route to the Spice Islands. There is no evidence that Magellan planned to sail around the world – his object was always the Spice Islands.

With his ships the *Trinidad, Concepcion, Victoria, San Antonio* and *Santiago*, he sailed westwards to the coast of South America. Near Rio de Janeiro the natives thought the ships were sea monsters and that the little boats were

The 16th Century map-makers represented the Straits of Magellan in this way.

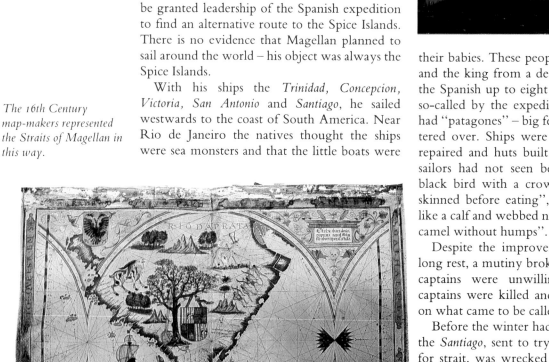

their babies. These people were happy to barter and the king from a deck of cards could secure the Spanish up to eight chickens. At Patagonia, so-called by the expedition because the people had "patagones" – big feet – the expedition wintered over. Ships were unloaded, beached and repaired and huts built. Among the sights the sailors had not seen before were "a flightless black bird with a crow's beak that had to be skinned before eating", "seawolves with heads like a calf and webbed nails at their sides" and "a camel without humps".

Despite the improvement in health and the long rest, a mutiny broke out when some of the captains were unwilling to continue. Two captains were killed and their bodies displayed on what came to be called Gallows Point.

Before the winter had set in at St Julians Bay, the *Santiago*, sent to try to discover the hoped-for strait, was wrecked on a sandbank and the crew scrambled to shore. The *Santiago* was lost and two men managed to walk the 72 miles (115 kilometres) back in freezing temperatures to bring word of the shipwreck. After four days they reached their base and the crew was saved.

Continuing the search southwards the remaining four ships entered the Cape of the Virgins or the Cape of the Eleven Thousand

Virgins of St. Ursula – and amidst great excitement discovered two days later the strait for which they had been searching. This tortuous passage took five weeks to traverse, battling through fjords and inlets against the wind, but the continuing salt water flowing through the channel assured the sailors that they were on the right track. They named the land to the south "Tierra del Fuego", because of the native fires they spied from their boats. When they reassembled the *San Antonio* was not among them and worried, the other crews left banners and messages as a trail. But the *San Antonio* had deserted taking with her most of the expedition's supplies.

As Magellan came out of the strait the sea before him was calm and he thus named it Mar Pacifico – the Pacific Ocean. At the end of November they set out optimistically in the belief that they would reach the nearby coast in a few weeks.

Unfortunately no land appeared, and food had to be severely rationed. They ate "only old biscuit turned to powder, all full of worms and stinking of the urine that the rats had made on it". Leather was cut into strips and left in the sea to soften, then grilled and eaten. The water was little more than bilge. Rats were caught and sold

at a handsome profit for food. The crew lost their teeth, their gums bled, their tongues turned black . . .

Nearly 100 days later after two unhelpful sightings the three remaining ships arrived at the Philippines with 150 survivors. Here pigs, fruit, fish, eggs and fresh water helped them regain their health.

Magellan had reached the east sailing westwards thus enabling future sailors to know the distance around the world.

Part of his mission was to convert the heathen and to ally the chiefs to the King of Spain. In support of a friendly chief he undertook a battle against a heathen king at Mactan, and needlessly met his end.

The friendly natives he was supporting looked on as some 60 of Magellan's armed men were landed from small boats into shallow waters. Before they reached the shore they were attacked by an estimated 1500 warriors and Magellan was killed.

Only one remaining ship left the Spice Islands with 47 men and 13 natives aboard heading for home alone. She arrived safely back on Tuesday 9th September 1522, with 18 survivors and four natives. Their cargo brought a handsome profit to their sponsors.

(Centre) Portuguese ships at the time of Magellan. They were elaborate vessels with a great volume of sail and very detailed and heavily decorated wood carving.

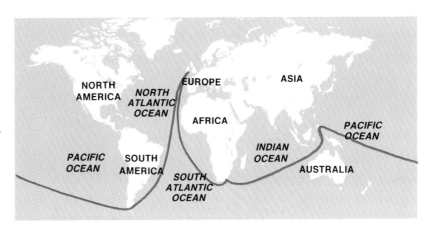

Amerigo Vespucci
(1454–1512)

Amerigo Vespucci was immortalized in the naming of America but little is known for certain about his voyages – he never commanded the expeditions he undertook and even the number of them is disputed.

We do know that he was an Italian – a Florentine banker from the Medici family – who like his countryman, Columbus (see page 20), served with the Portuguese and Spanish.

In the latter half of the 15th century Portugal and Spain were a honeypot for adventurers who hoped to make their fortunes through trade with the East. Vespucci relates in his letters that he sailed from Cadiz in 1497 "towards the Great Gulf of the Ocean Sea". This may have been under the command of Hojeda in a Castilian expedition which probably landed at Rio Grande do Norte. He was also reputed to have reached Honduras and the Mexican coast and to

have brought back with him 222 slaves.

In this second voyage, when the Portuguese King Manuel sent three caravels (see page 18) to explore Brazil, he explored the Amazon River. He also appears to have explored the Brazilian coast from 8°S to 32°S until he had to turn back because of the cold and bad weather. Vespucci relates that they found nothing of any value except for "dye-wood trees and cassia and the tree that makes negrol and other marvels that cannot be described". His purpose was obviously to sail as far south as possible.

In January 1502, on the third expedition he discovered the bay which he called Rio de Janeiro (River of January). In 1503 a fort was established in southern Brazil and dye-wood was exported to Portugal. He had also found Port St. Julian, some 20 years before Magellan (see page 26), the port which was to be the site of bloodshed and the punishment of mutiny on two distinctive occasions. If Vespucci had sailed another 2° south he would have come to what is now the Magellan Straits.

While he believed he had touched the extreme coast of Asia, he also referred to "Mundus Novus" – the New World – and when the idea grew in Europe that a whole new continent had been discovered it was suggested it be called America and the name appeared on a map in 1507. If Columbus had used the word "novus" instead of "otro mundo" – "other world" as he did, he may well have had the honour of the continent being named after him instead!

Although Vespucci had made his voyages for Portugal he returned to Spain and he must there have influenced the cartography and the exploration of that time.

Detail of an illustrated map of "Mundus Novus" – the New World – made after Vespucci's voyages.

Sir Francis Drake

(c.1540–1596)

The legendary Drake, a bold, swashbuckling servant of Elizabeth I of England would perhaps be frowned on today for his adventures. He was, after all, primarily a pirate in the service of Elizabeth (or privateer as he was more politely called), attacking and plundering Spanish ships for their gold and booty. Today, when we are all aware of the need for conservation, it seems shocking to learn he killed 3000 penguins on one day for food, and on another, 300 seals an hour for provisions.

However, these were different times, and Drake, his early life having made him ambitious to beat the Spanish, and to gain gold, became England's greatest hero. Spain and Portugal had dominated the world's trade routes. Drake was to point the way towards England's place as a world power and destroy Spain's and Portugal's monopoly of the Pacific Ocean. England had profited little from the resulting expansion of trade.

Francis Drake was said to have had a modest background, and had learned his sailing on coastal vessels around the Thames. He did, however, have rich relations, and with his cousin, John Hawkins, he travelled towards the Gulf of Mexico, where a Spanish attack sowed the seeds of hatred he was to feel ever after for the Spanish.

He had no qualms in spending the next ten years plundering the Spaniards in the West Indies and on the Spanish Main.

When he was in his early thirties he attacked the Spanish Treasury at Nombre de Dios in Panama, where he found an enormous store of silver, worth nearly a million pounds sterling. He was so badly wounded in the attack that his crew couldn't believe any man could lose so much blood and still live. This wound caused him to faint, and the English withdrew. So the silver was not taken: nevertheless he took back some £40,000 worth of booty.

On this trip, while he was at Panama, some friendly natives, who were guiding him, showed him a tall tree with steps cut into it. From the top one could see the seas to the south as well as the Atlantic, and Drake asked God's blessing in a venture he wanted to accomplish to "sail once in an English ship in that sea", or, in other words, to sail round the world.

On an expedition five years later he would sail in that sea, where the Spanish had many coastal outposts. When he set out with five ships and 164 crew, the men were not told where they were heading until after they had passed Cape Verde Islands.

Condemned to Death

From Cape Verde, having already captured Spanish and Portuguese vessels on the way, they made for Brazil, reaching it after 54 days' sailing. After stopping at the River Plate to rendezvous with his ships, he made for Port St. Julian, just as his predecessor, Magellan had done more than 50 years before (see page 26). Here history repeated itself, when one of Drake's captains, Doughty, was accused of mutiny and condemned to death. There are many varying accounts of this incident. One account states – "After the trial Drake and Doughty knelt side by side to receive Holy Communion, dined together then parted: Doughty to his execution, Drake to continue sailing round the world" – and although Drake was criticized for his actions, it must have been accepted as legitimate, since he was never asked to account for his decision.

For Drake, still following in Magellan's footsteps, the Strait was as hazardous as it had been for the latter. The land rises high on both sides and the mountains are snow-covered. There are deep fjords and many blind turnings. As he entered the Straits he changed the name of his ship, the *Pelican*, to the *Golden Hind*. This was now one of three remaining ships, the other two having been abandoned earlier. They took only 16 days to sail through the straits, but instead of the peaceful "Pacific" that awaited Magellan, they sailed into a tremendous storm which forced them southwards and kept them sailing for 52 days. They were forced southwards as far as 57°, and eventually found safety in the southern islands. They were not blown as far as Cape Horn, but Drake guessed that there was a passage from the Atlantic to the Pacific, which would discount the theory of there being a vast continent stretching south from Tierra del Fuego.

Drake was now alone with his crew of the *Golden Hind*. The other two ships had disappeared and he sought for them along the western coast of South America, plundering the Spanish ships he encountered along the way. One had so much cargo it took a number of days to transfer it to the *Golden Hind*.

Off one island, Mocha, Drake sent two of his men to get fresh water and, thinking they were Spaniards, the natives killed them. Drake was wounded again here, this time in the face.

Drake, no doubt well pleased with his revenge and his booty, began to think of returning home, but he was aware that the Spanish might well be waiting to relieve him of his spoils in the Magellan Straits. He decided to cross the Pacific instead and return via the East Indies and the Cape of Good Hope.

In his search for a good wind, Drake sailed north and reached the beautiful natural harbour of the Bay of San Francisco. He may well have thought of continuing further to try to reach the Atlantic via the north, but decided against it, when his men were obviously wary of the high latitudes. The land was taken in Elizabeth's name as the Spanish did not appear to have made any claims here, and the friendly natives danced and presented Drake with a crown of feathers. The crew gave out medicines and treatment to the natives, and a monument was set up.

(Right) The Armada tapestry showing both the Spanish and English fleets locked in combat.

"Oysters on Trees"

Then they headed eastwards, first to the Philippines, then the Moluccas, where a local king greeted them with much ceremony in his canoes. He came aboard and was enchanted by the playing of the English musicians.

The *Golden Hind* nearly foundered on a rock off the Celebes, and only a strong gusty gale forced them off. After taking on board some spices, including valuable cloves, they sailed via the Cape of Good Hope – "the fairest cape . . . in the whole circumference of the earth", to Sierra Leone, where they reported seeing many elephants and "oysters growing on trees" – coconuts?

Like Magellan's ships the journey had taken three years, but, unlike Magellan, Drake lived to

his final historic exploit came in the first great English victory at sea – the defeat of the Spanish Armada.

It is said that he was heard to say he had time to finish the game of bowls he was playing before defeating the Armada, which had been sighted off the Lizard. Whether or not he actually did say it he certainly chased them northwards, where many, already damaged, were then shipwrecked.

Unfortunately even the man, whose courage and good leadership made him such a popular hero, was later criticized for his failure against the Portuguese in an attack in which many of his own men died. Also, when he next attacked the West Indies the Spanish were more than ready for him with their strong defences.

Drake contracted dysentery on this trip, and, probably demoralized by his lack of success, died off Porto Bello, He was buried at sea in a lead coffin and his drum was returned to his family home at Buckland Abbey. There is a legend that the drum will sound every time England is in danger.

(**Below**) *Detail from a contemporary map.*

receive the understandably great honours that were heaped on him. He had gained £47 for every £ invested in the expedition, and the Queen came aboard at Deptford and proclaimed him a knight of the realm. The *Golden Hind* later became a holiday resort, and a dining and drinking room well into the 17th Century. One person suggested that she be put on top of St. Paul's Church instead of the steeple, but today all that remains is a chair, which is in the Bodleian Library at Oxford.

Drake's circumnavigation was not the pinnacle of his glamorous career. He went on to command the fleet sent against the Spanish in the Caribbean. As General of Her Majesty's Navy he burned and plundered further and then sank and burned 33 ships in the harbour at Cadiz. But

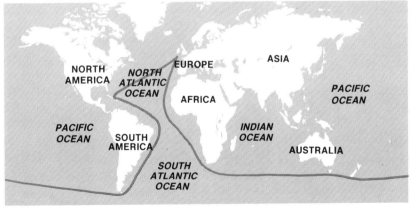

Sir Martin Frobisher

(c.1535–1594)

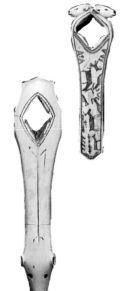

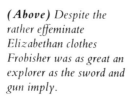

(Above) Despite the rather effeminate Elizabethan clothes Frobisher was as great an explorer as the sword and gun imply.

(Left and opposite) Although the materials for craftsmanship were very limited the fine designs on these arrow-straighteners are extremely delicate. They have changed little and are very similar to the type produced by the Eskimo in Frobisher's time.

Frobisher has been called a tough, selfish adventurer rather than a great commander and explorer, man "trained in a rough school whose highest ideal was courage, tempered by piracy", but his continued belief in a northwest passage to Asia and his persistent efforts to find it in the face of opposition and terrible climatic conditions surely earns for him his place among the great explorers.

He was a contemporary of Drake and fought with him as Vice-Admiral in the 1585 raid in the West Indies, and we have a good account of his explorations told to a chronicler of his time.

Serving Queen Elizabeth, he gained experience as a seaman and must have listened to the stories of sailors who had been to the East. He was determined to look for a Northwest Passage to India and the Indies, and tried to get support for his venture from London merchants. Eventually some of Elizabeth's court helped to finance him, and he collected enough money to buy three small ships, two of some 25 tons each (the *Gabriel* and the *Michael*), and a 10 ton pinnace. He took with him such navigational instruments as were in use, geography books, Mercator's map and a sundial, and in 1576 after a short trip the *Gabriel*, and *Michael* and the pinnace sighted land. However, the bad conditions they were to encounter time and again prevented their going too close and the pinnace was lost in a storm. After some time the *Michael* headed for home, erroneously reporting the loss of the *Gabriel*. Though the weather continued to be bad Frobisher kept on, convinced he would find the passage. At one stage his top mast was blown overboard. Undaunted, he eventually came upon a strait between two lands. At first he could not cross it because of the winds and ice, but the ice was later blown away. Frobisher thought it had been carried away by currents and that the landmasses rising high on either side of him as he sailed some 50 leagues on (a league is about three miles or 1.9 kilometres) were those of America on the portside and Asia on the starboard. He was, in fact, sailing up what is now known as Frobisher Bay on Baffin Island.

After initial suspicion the Eskimo brought him fresh food. Bells, looking glasses and trinkets were exchanged for furs. Lulled into a feeling of security a party of men went ashore and

ORBIS TERRAE COMPENDIOSA DESCRIPTIO
Quam ex Magna Vniuersali Gerardi Mercatoris Domino Richardo Gartho, Geographic ac cçterarum bonarum artium amatori ac fautori summe, in veteris amicitiç ac familiaritatis memoriã Rumoldus Mercator fieri curabat Aº M.D.lxxxvii.

were captured by the Eskimo to disappear for ever.

Gold Deposits Discovered

While the men had been ashore they had collected specimens of flora and samples of rock. Among them was a piece of black stone which Frobisher casually included among his samples. He showed little interest in it although it seemed to contain a kind of metal. It would have been better had he thrown it away as it was to cause a stir on his return.

He arrived back, and convinced Queen Elizabeth and her people that he had found the sought-after passage. The piece of stone which had apparently shone like gold when put into a fire was sent away to assayers for testing, one of whom claimed it contained rich gold.

Now there were plenty of people to support a further venture, and although Frobisher did not give up hope of continuing the search for a way through to the East, the search for gold became the prime object. This time he was lent a tall ship of over 100 tons by Elizabeth and given £1000 for the expedition. He was given the title of "High Admiral of all seas, countries, lands, isles, as well of Cathay as all places of new discovery". With the new ship, *Aid*, and the two small ships of his previous voyage – the *Gabriel* and *Michael* – he set off with his crew, soldiers and gentlemen. This second trip was longer against the heavy winds, and even in July there were icebergs. On a nearby hill, after their arrival, they formally took possession. Over the next weeks they remained wary of the local inhabitants, although they usually appeared to be friendly. Frobisher tried to take one of the Eskimo aboard as an interpreter, and an understandable skirmish followed. Frobisher described the Eskimo as "like Tartars, with long blacke haire, broad faces and flatter noses, and tawnie in colour, wearing seale skinnes". The women had "blewe streekes down the cheeks, and round about the eyes".

On this voyage they came across an English shirt and doublet and some shoes, and were hopeful that the prisoners taken on the first voyage by the Eskimo might still be alive, but

Mercator's map of the world – the first map to show the Tropics and the Equator.

Frobisher's ships look unbelievably fragile in this artist's interpretation of the arctic regions. It is difficult to imagine how the crews could even attempt to survive in such hostile regions for so long.

they never discovered them.

By the end of August they had enough of the ore to return and thankful they were to do so. The ice was already beginning to pack them in, and their clothes were in ruins and their tools no longer fit to work with. Bad weather continued to dog them and on one occasion two men were swept off the *Gabriel.* They managed to pull the boatswain in, but the master was lost. On another, men had to work partly underwater to repair the rudder of the *Aid* and to hear them described as half dead could have been no exaggeration in those freezing waters. Frobisher had most of the "gold ore" locked up in Bristol Castle before he went off to report to the Queen.

Encouraged by further tests on the ore, Frobisher was asked to return yet again.

This time the plan was to establish a fort in the Bay. It was prebuilt and would be large enough for a hundred sailors, miners and soldiers. Three ships were to remain on site, and the other 12 readied for the voyage would carry back the ore after a summer of mining.

Knowing now of the dangers of these hostile waters, Admiral Frobisher insisted on a strict moral code of conduct; that ships should stay close together behind the admiral ship; that warnings be given from ship to ship in fog; prearranged signals should be used and even a code. On the call "Before the world was God" a reply

"After God came Christ" was to be given.

Despite these elaborate preparations the ice and storms were so dangerous that when the ships finally found each other again after dreadful experiences of being thrown up by the ice, losing each other in heavy fogs, and coming within inches of "mountains of ice", they wanted to return home. Frobisher would not give up, however, and pushing their way through blinding snow they finally reached harbour. There was no hope of erecting the fort – too much of it had been lost in the battle with the storms – so they decided to fill the ships and hasten for home, although Frobisher did make one more attempt to find his passage in a small pinnace.

What a bitter disappointment it must have been for Frobisher when they returned after this third trip to discover that their precious gold was only iron pyrites. A lot of money had been lost, and, as well, no strait had been found.

Although Frobisher had not found his passage he went onto become one of the leading sea commanders of the time. He was given a knighthood after his skill in charge of the *Triumph* during the battle with the Spanish Armada. Like Drake he swelled the English coffers by his piracy of the Spanish treasure fleets, and like many adventurers of the time, he met his end violently after being wounded in a battle near Brest while attacking a fort.

*(**Below**) The Eskimo attack on Frobisher at Baffin Island. What the Eskimo lacked in more sophisticated weapons, they made up for in their numbers.*

*(**Above**) Detail of contemporary map featuring "creatures of the sea" found in the arctic regions.*

William Barents

(sometimes Barentz, c1550–1597)

This artist's impression of the hut which Barents and his crew built at Novaya Zemlya shows it as being a fairly comfortable, weatherproof construction. It also shows the men wearing basic heavy outdoor clothing which could be considered by arctic explorers to be totally inadequate today.

Towards the end of the 16th Century expeditions to the Arctic were being undertaken first by the English and then by the Dutch to try to find an alternative route to China and the Spice Islands. At that time the Portuguese controlled the eastern route from Europe, the Spanish the western. A northern way would avoid confrontation with these nations and would, besides, be a shorter route.

In June 1594 Barents travelled as pilot with instructions to "navigate in North Seas and discover the kingdoms of China and Cathay to the North of Norway and Muscovy towards Tartary". A month after setting out, the party reached Novaya Zemlya and although the ice hindered their progress, Barents reached the north part of the island, crossing the sea which is now named after him.

Their second voyage was not as successful as the first and the seven ships laden with cargoes of merchandise to exchange for spices made less progress than on the first. Barents though, was a fine navigator and, using the position of the sun, was able to calculate exactly where they were.

The Return to Novaya Zemlya

Barent's third voyage set off from Amsterdam in May 1596 with Barents as chief pilot under Captain Heenskerck in one of the two ships, the other ship being captained by a Jan Cornelison Rijp. The later was forced to turn back after a few months, but Barents' ship was to go on and its men were to find themselves closed in (frozen in a sea of ice) for the whole of an Arctic winter.

By early June the thick ice was already preventing their passage onward and they were encountering the bears who were to prove such a danger and a nuisance on the trip. One which they killed had a skin 12 feet (3.7 metres) long and it was on this trip that they named Bear Island after their encounters. The crew ate red geese and "seamew's eggs", on one occasion collecting 60,000 eggs.

When they first reached Novaya Zemlya the weather was too bad for them to land and they continued to be troubled by bears. By the end of August they were being hemmed in by the ice so much that the ship began to crack "which was fearful to see and hear and made all the hair of our heads to rise upright with fear". These were the words of one Gerritt de Veer who was to keep an accurate record of the next miserable months and to leave us with a memorable picture of the hardships and ingenuity of the Dutch explorers.

A Winter Refuge

When the ship was closed in by the ice, the crew carried their boats and provisions onto the land and used an old sail to make a tent. At this stage (early September) they were still hopeful that they would be able to get away but they soon realized that they needed to plan to winter over. They found driftwood, tree roots and timber and set to to build the house seen here in the picture. They had by this time one casualty, the carpenter, but they soon built their shelter and carried everything they needed from the ship.

The bears which plagued them throughout their expedition were useful in providing fat to light their lamp, although all the party was later to become ill when they dined on the bear's livers.

The ship's doctor made a bath out of a wine cask. They caught foxes both to eat and to provide them with fur for hats and they almost all suffocated on one occasion when they brought coal from the ship, stopped up all the draughts in their house and made an enormous fire.

After weather that was clear and stormy in turns they had a calm patch when they dug their way out of the house on January 5th, Twelfth Night. To celebrate the date they made pancakes and drank to the Three Kings and pretended that they were at home.

When the weather was not too bad they played ball outside to keep fit and even devised a game of golf.

At last the days began to lengthen and they caught glimpses of the open sea, and as the men were beginning to get impatient Barents promised that if the ship were not free by the end of May, they would set out in their two open boats. This they did.

When they left in the two boats, with sails made from the ship, they took with them some bread, cheese, bacon, oil and wine. Barents was suffering from scurvy and a week later, shortly after he had asked for a drink, he died.

Their homeward passage was not an easy one – they were nearly crushed by ice, they had to drag their boats over icebergs, and they had to fight against the marauding bears.

At last with a strong wind to blow them west they eventually met two Russian ships. You can imagine their delight after 13 months of only their own company and that of the bears. The Russian crew fed them and they were excited to meet up again with Jan Cornelison Rijp. They joined his ship and arrived in Amsterdam in early November.

Two hundred and seventy-five years later the house that they had built was re-discovered and many of the items they used over that long winter were still preserved. Within a few more years part of the account which Barents had written, hidden in a powder horn and put up the chimney of the house, was recovered.

One of the navigational instruments which allowed Barents to be such an accurate navigator.

Henry Hudson

(c1570–1611)

There is something especially heroic about an explorer who dies in pursuit of his goal. Henry Hudson was like another famous polar explorer, Captain Oates, (a member of Scott's Antarctic Expedition) in this respect; he disappeared into the snowy wastes and was never seen again.

In the well-known portrait shown here Hudson sits at the tiller of the small boat in which he was abandoned, with his son gazing up at him, and the look on his face of a man who is prepared to die.

Hudson's first recorded voyage in 1607 was in search of the North Pole. The theory was that there was a clear route over the Pole to Cathay and the "islands of spicery". When the Spanish and Portuguese had discovered that tropical seas were not hot to boiling point, as has been thought, it was suggested that Arctic waters may not be so cold either. Hudson was to find otherwise, and was eventually forced back after reaching Spitzbergen.

A year later he was back again – this time in a vain search for the North East Passage along Russia's Arctic coast.

Another failure the following year, when his crew rebelled off the coast of Novaya Zemlya, led to an "alternative" journey across the Atlantic which put his name on the map for the first time.

Reports of the existence of a string of Great Lakes in the interior of North America had led to speculation that there might be a passage to the Pacific in the latitude 40°N. Perhaps Hudson mistook the Manna-hata River for this strait, for he sailed up it for 150 miles (240 kilometres) before turning back near the position where Albany, New York State, now stands. The river is now called after him and the island at which the Manna-hata River began was to be bought from the Indians only 17 years later for $24-worth of cloth and beads.

His final attempt at the North West Passage was to end in tragedy. In the *Discovery* which was as fine a ship as his crew was quarrelsome, he sailed through the Strait and into the Bay which are both named after him. As he sailed due south 400 miles (640 kilometres), he could have been forgiven for thinking that he had really found the legendary passage to the East. However, September found him at the southern end of the bay with nowhere to go but north, and winter closing in. Huddled in makeshift shelters, the winter passed miserably for the crew, with several deaths from scurvy and starvation. Resentment against Hudson grew. He had already replaced one mate with another after a quarrel, and was now suspected of hoarding supplies. When Spring came and Hudson showed no signs of wanting to leave the bay, resentment turned to mutiny. On 23 June 1611 there was a struggle in which four men died. Hudson, his son John and six others were put into a small boat which was then cut adrift.

The only question that remains is how long Hudson and his companions took to die. Twenty years later a Bristol sailor reported signs of a European-style hut on an island near the site of the mutiny. And there is a story handed down by the Inuit (Eskimo) of Hudson Bay of the first white man they ever saw. He was dead, but the boy in the boat with him was still alive. What became of him was not recalled.

Few of the mutinous crew, and none of the ringleaders, survived the return journey, so none of the survivors were charged with mutiny when they arrived back in England.

Hudson's achievements were founded on failure. By failing, in spite of all efforts to find either a North East or a North West Passage, he showed to those who followed that the route to the East, if it existed at all, would not be an easy one.

(**Left**) *John Collier's painting "Hudson's Last Voyage" throws into relief the bravery of those who explored the arctic wastes. The scale of the terrain dwarfed the men who were grossly ill-equipped to make such a venture.*

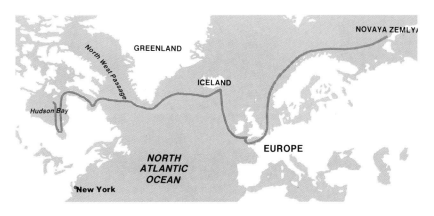

Abel Janszoon Tasman

(c.1603–1659)

Abel Janszoon Tasman and his wife – taken from a contempory portrait.
(Centre) *The islands of Moa and Insou as drawn by Tasman himself.*

By the early part of the 17th Century the Dutch had proven themselves to be great traders and Amsterdam was one of the richest cities on earth. Their "Company of Far Lands", later to be called the Dutch East India Company (DEIC), had enabled them to establish themselves in the East Indies. They chased away the Spanish fleets and controlled a vast spice empire.

At this time there was a wide belief in the existence of a vast continent stretching from the South Pole into the tropics and although Dutch sailors has explored parts of the south and west coasts of Australia it was not known if the coasts were continental and whether they were connected with the southern continent.

Abel Tasman, born near Groningen in Holland, received enough education to be able to write and to become a skilled navigator, and after sailing as an able seaman rose quickly to the rank of the master then "commandeur". In 1632 or 1633 he captained the *Mocha* for the Dutch East India Company.

After an unsuccessful voyage to find a rich country inhabited by friendly and civilized people, somewhere eastwards at 37° North, having discovered nothing and lost half the crew through sickness, he came to the attention of the

Governor of the DEIC, Anthony Van Diemen. The Governor supported a venture to sail further south in the Indian Ocean than anyone had yet done to investigate whether the southern continent reached the Antarctic. Tasman was also asked to investigate the "practicability of a sea passage east to Chile, rediscover the Solomons and explore New Guinea". Van Diemen wanted to piece together the information collected between 1616 and 1628 and find out more about Australia's relationship to the southern continent.

In 1642 Tasman sailed for Mauritius with the *Heemskerk* and the *Zeehaen*. He was also required to "snatch rich booty from the Castilians" sailing south into the higher latitudes of the southern Indian Ocean.

After sailing through the "Roaring Forties" as far as the Australian Bight the ships sighted the southern tip of Tasmania at the end of November. They could see high land and dense forests and though they saw no natives there were signs of habitation. Tasman discussed further plans with his officers and views and votes were floated between one boat and another. It was decided not to sail up the west coast of Tasmania (which they then called Van Diemen's Land), so that they never discovered the Bass Strait. They sailed instead towards New

Zealand, having planted the Dutch flag ashore on Tasmania. This was done by a carpenter who swam ashore with it in a sea-swell too heavy to allow Tasman to land. Also, a landing party had been put off earlier by hearing shrill singing noises and had gone back on board.

Encounter at Murderers Bay

When Tasman landed on the west coast of the South Island of New Zealand he thought he had found the coast of the southern continent. His explorations were cut short by a Maori attack: "One of the boats was attacked by Southlanders who approaching made a fearful noise, and treated the seven sailors in such a way that they beat four to death with long staffs . . . After committing this murder, they rowed with incredible skilfulness to the shore so that before the Dutchmen could use the guns, they were out of range". Tasman named this spot on the west coast of New Zealand's North Island "Murderers Bay".

On his way back to Batavia, as Jakarta was then called, he discovered the friendly islanders of Tonga and Fiji, and he stopped at New Guinea.

By the time they returned in under a year they had travelled 5000 miles (8000 kilometres) and had lost only 10 men from illness, but the DEIC were not pleased. Tasman had found no rich trade and had not been investigative enough, despite the fact that he had sailed right round Australia, although he had not seen it.

A year later he mapped the western and northern coasts of Australia, but still found no riches.

In 1648 when Tasman was commanding eight ships against the Spanish in the Philippines he disgraced himself by almost murdering two sailors whom he found away from quarters without leave. He had dined and wined too well and punished the first one by putting a halter round his neck, and then trying to hang the second. Tasman was later tried for attempted hanging and severely punished and publicly humiliated.

He was obviously a fine sailor, and although not a great thinker, had zest for exploration. His care, combined with his courage and energy, helped in two very important discoveries.

He went on to stay in Batavia for 15 years after his return from the 1644 voyage, during which time he not only fought the Spaniards, but also was in command of a trading venture to what was then Siam – now Thailand.

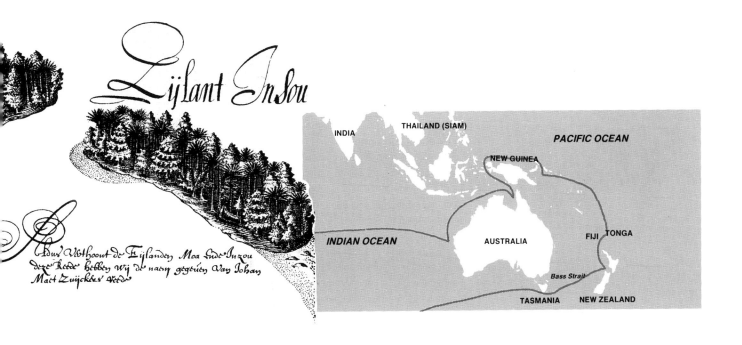

The wildlife of Botany Bay impressed Cook with the brilliant colours of the birds and strange shapes of the plants.

Cook has been described as the "last of the great early navigators and the first of the modern scientific explorers", and there is hardly anyone in the western world today who has not at least heard of him. His accurate mapping and the extent of his travels presented the world as it is, and apart from the Polar regions and some of the small details we could use the work of the last ten years of his life today.

His story is one we all love to hear – that of starting at the bottom and rising to great fame and importance.

One of nine children, his first job as a twelve-year-old was as a grocer's boy near Whitby, although he had been to school where he learned writing and arithmetic, but he could not wait to leave. The romance of seafaring called and after an apprenticeship and some trading in the Baltic, he joined the Royal Navy. He had already started to learn navigation and he "had a mind to try his fortune that way".

While the work he did in the first 40 years of his life was very valuable – he spent much of his time surveying the St. Lawrence and other parts of Canada, and indeed had taken part in the capture of the French in Quebec during the Seven Years War (1756–1763) – it was the last ten years of his life that were to give him the reputation of great explorer.

Cook was appointed commander of an

expedition by the Royal Society (a learned body set up to further the cause of science) to go to the South Pacific to watch the "Transit of Venus" – the passage of the planet Venus across the face of the Sun. The observation could help in measuring the earth's distance from the sun. There was another reason for the trip. It was still thought that an enormous landmass the size of Europe and Asia together must stretch from the south up into the tropics to counterbalance the land north of the equator.

Under Sealed Instructions

So in 1768 he set out in the coalship *Endeavour* with a natural scientist named Joseph Banks, Daniel Solander a naturalist, and the Royal Society astronomer, Charles Green, to observe Venus and find the Southern continent. Instructions for the second stage of his trip were given in an "inclosed Sealed Packet".

Rounding the tip of South America at Tierra del Fuego they stopped in gales and bitter cold to collect botanical specimens, then went on in calm seas to round Cape Horn.

There were two problems that dogged the sailors of the time – the inability to determine longitude and the heavy toll taken by scurvy. Cook was helped in his explorations by the knowledge passed on by Green's superior at the Royal Society in the use of the sextant to find longitude; and Cook's insistence on the crew eating fresh food helped guard against scurvy. Cook took citrus juice and sauerkraut: " I found it necessary to put every one on board to an Allowance; for such are the Tempers and disposissions (sic) of seamen in general that whatever you give them out of the common way altho' it be ever so much for their good it will not go down with them and you will hear nothing but murmurings gainest the Man that first invented it; but the Moment they see their superiors set a Value upon it, it becomes the finest stuff in the World, and the inventor a damn'd finest fellow."

When the *Endeavour* reached Tahiti they built a fort (Fort Venus) to observe the planet, and when there was trouble between the Tahitians and the Europeans Cook punished his own men severely in front of the Tahitians. On one occasion he lashed the ship's butcher after he had threatened a Tahitian girl while the Tahitians looking on tearfully pleaded for mercy. Pilfering by the Tahitians was something of a problem for the party and the daring of one of them was such that he stole Cook's stockings from under his pillow while he was on his bed and awake.

When the boat left Tahiti it had on board a Tahitian chief, Tupia, and a servant, who were to be interpreters in the voyage ahead. Cook made for New Zealand where he encountered unfriendly Maoris who were, reputedly, cannibals. The party spent six months there and sailed some 2400 miles (3800 kilometres) around the beautiful and fertile North and South Islands. From there they sailed westwards to the southeast coast of Australia to what they called Botany Bay, because of its many plants. Cook's high opinion of the place was to lead later to English criminals being conscripted to settle there. Here, too, they were not welcomed by the Aborigines, and their gifts evoked no response. On their way northwards through the

On his second visit to Tahiti, Cook's ships were greeted by local people in small boats who rowed out to meet him.

dangerous Great Barrier Reef, despite Cook's navigational skills, they struck a reef. They managed to get off and when they beached the *Endeavour* for repairs they discovered that the coral rock had actually broken off and plugged the ship.

By the time the ship reached what is now Jakarta nearly all the crew was ill with either dysentery or malaria. Despite Cook's greatly improved standards of cleanliness and his efforts to provide a healthy diet seven of his crew died so that he had to take on more hands at Cape Town. Although by the time they returned to

Sailing near Antarctica, Cook's ships Resolution and Adventure stopped to take ice on board in order to melt it down for fresh water.

England three years after they had set out they had lost 35 out of their 85 men, this was considerably less than many other voyages of the day.

A year and a day after his return Cook set out again with astronomers, naturalists and artists in the two ships, *Resolution* and *Adventure* on the search for the vast southern continent. In mid-January 1773 for the first time in history, and sailing from the west, they crossed the Antarctic Circle and a year later sailed eastwards south of New Zealand to 71°S. This proved that while there was ice and maybe some land around the South Pole there was no continent comparable with Eurasia. Although Cook did not know it he came within 75 miles (120 kilometres) of Antarctica. The conditions through which he had sailed in 1773 were described as an almost

perpetual combination of fog, rain or sleet, strong gales and an ice-studded sea; a year later when he reached the record 71° 10′ South the weather was clear, but they had made their way through icebergs standing up to 200 feet (60 metres) above water, and they now saw before them great mounds of ice like a ridge of mountains. Behind that ice-barrier may well have been the coastline of Antarctica.

Massacred by Cannibals

Heading back north, Cook became ill and when he was recovering he had a yearning for fresh meat. As there was none on the ship a pet dog was killed and "served up at table".

Cook sailed for Queen Charlotte's Sound in New Zealand, and looked for the *Adventure* which had become separated from the *Resolution*. He found signs of it but it was not until after he returned to England that he learned that the crew had been massacred and some of them eaten.

After further exploration in the Pacific and Antarctic (going as far as the Amundsen Sea), they stopped on their way home toward Plymouth at Easter Island, where they saw the mysterious giant statues. At this point they had been 104 days out of sight of land. By the time they reached home only one man had died of disease, despite the great lengths of time at sea and the hardships with which they had to contend. They had sailed 70,000 miles (112,000 kilometres) in the three years they had taken to sail round the world from west to east. Cook was honoured by the Royal Society for his achievements.

His last voyage was to try to find a passage from the Pacific to the Atlantic around North America from the west to east. He sailed again in the *Resolution* and was accompanied by Charles Clerke, captaining the *Discovery*. His route past the Cape of Good Hope via Tasmania and New Zealand, Tahiti and the Sandwich Islands (now Hawaiian Islands) took him through the Bering Strait to Northern Alaska where ice blocked his passage further. It was not a good year and he was forced to return, although he had made useful exchanges with some Russian traders who, despite their not having a language in common, had given him information for map-making.

When they got back to the Sandwich islands

and anchored at Kealakekua the natives honoured Cook greatly. They thought, apparently, that he was a reincarnation of one of their mythical half-hero, half-gods. However, when he returned a week or so later the natives, although friendly, seemed "less cordial".

When the *Discovery's* cutter was stolen Cook tried to take the island's King as hostage against its return. The King was well treated and agreed to go with the Europeans, but his wife held on to him and shrieked that he would be killed if he went onto the ship. This led to the islanders throwing stones so that Cook's men fired their muskets and a fight broke out. When Cook was last seen he was standing at the edge of the water trying to urge his own men to stop firing. He was stabbed in the back and fell into the water where he was held down, taken ashore and clubbed, slashed and stabbed.

Later some of his remains were presented to Captain Clerke who took over as leader of the expedition, and until the islanders were converted to Christianity 50 years later they were said to have carried the rest of Cook's remains around the island once a year in a wicker basket covered with red feathers. It was an ignominious end for the scientist, navigator, cartographer and sailor, who had done so much to improve sailing conditions for his crew and to increase so widely the knowledge of the globe.

The islanders surround Cook before stabbing, drowning and finally clubbing him to death.

The small statuette is from Hawaii and depicts a Hawaiian god.

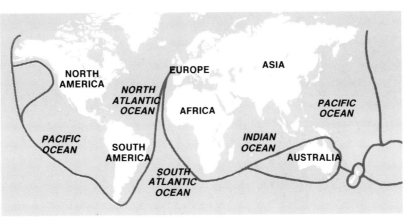

Charles Darwin

(1809–1882)

Tanagra Darwini, a bird first discovered by Charles Darwin on his travels and named after him.

The most familiar image of Charles Darwin is that of a white-bearded old man with beetle brows and a gloomy expression.

This is based on photographs of him taken in his old age, when he suffered a good deal from ill health. For the last forty years of his life he lived a semi-invalid life in a large house deep in the country. There he conducted scientific research and wrote up his findings, the most famous of which was his *Theory of Evolution*.

There is also a portrait of a much younger Darwin which shows the innocent face of a man in love with life and thirsting for adventure.

He was a poor scholar but he was fascinated by nature and loved being in the countryside collecting and recording. He also loved hunting and shooting!

Having failed to last the course at medical school, he was persuaded that the Church was his best chance of a career.

He might well have become a popular country parson who rode to hounds and collected beetles as a hobby if a letter from his old Cambridge professor had not arrived, offering him the chance to join the crew of *HMS Beagle* as the ship's naturalist. The aim of the voyage would be to extend a naval survey of South America, which had already begun in 1826, and to sail around the world making chronometrical measurements as it went (to help work out lines of longitude).

In spite of opposition from his father he eventually found himself waiting impatiently for the ship to leave Plymouth, which it finally did on 27 December 1831.

He wrote later: "The voyage of the *Beagle* has been by far the most important event in my life and has determined my whole career."

The Captain of the ship was a young aristocrat, Robert Fitzroy, who allowed Darwin to share his cabin with him. This was a mixed blessing as Fitzroy was an unpredictable, moody man and Darwin never knew when he might offend him.

As the ship tossed about in the Bay of Biscay, Darwin made an important personal discovery – he was a rotten sailor, so much so that he was seasick most of the time on the voyage. Luckily for him the *Beagle* stopped off at various places on the way for many weeks at a time. It was during these long periods when the ship was at anchor that Darwin realized the full possibilities of using the voyage for recording wonderful sights and collecting strange creatures.

Their first landfall in South America was at Bahia where Darwin saw his first tropical forest. Many years later he was to write: "The glories of the vegetation of the Tropics rise before my mind at the present time more vividly than anything else."

Skeletons of Creatures

It was further down the coast, on the bleak coast of Patagonia, that Darwin made the first of the discoveries that was to set his mind working towards his famous theory. Embedded in a low cliff of shingle and gravel he found the skeletons of creatures now extinct; a giant sloth, a giant armadillo and an animal much like a modern

Birds Pl. 47

Rhea Darwinii

Another bird discovered by Darwin and named after him was the Rhea Darwinii. Unfortunately, at Rio Negro, one of his party had killed and eaten it before realizing that it was rare. It was reconstructed from the remains and a sketch made of it.

hippopotamus. There was even the skeleton of a horse, which had not existed in South America when the Spanish arrived. All these creatures were related to modern animals, which showed that it was likely that animal species changed in shape over long periods of time. However, this was not what most Christians believed in those days. They thought that all the animals in the world had survived unchanged since Noah's Flood and that all extinct animals had perished in the Flood and could not be related to them.

The other idea that was impressed on him by his travels through the jungles and the Pampas of South America was that of the survival of the fittest. In the jungle both animals and plants had adopted all sorts of wonderful tricks in order to survive either by developing ingenious means of attack or by disguising themselves in order to prevent attack. Even among people themselves there was a struggle for survival going on, with the Europeans waging a one-sided war against the Indians who were being gradually wiped out.

Later on, when they had rounded Cape Horn and Darwin was exploring the Andes he came across fossil sea shells 12,000 feet (3660 metres) above sea level. He realized that these mountains must have taken a huge span of time to rise up from the sea bed. This too was contrary to the view of most Christians, who thought that the world was only five thousand years old.

It was on the next port of call that Darwin met with the evidence that was to prove to him that evolution was the result of a process of "natural selection".

The Galapagos Islands

The Galapagos Islands are a group of volcanic islands almost on the Equator. Being of fairly recent origin their wild life consisted of only a limited number of birds and reptiles which had adapted to their environment in a variety of ways which would not have happened if there had been more competition from other animals. There were finches, for example, some of whose beaks had adapted to cracking nuts and others to feeding on fruits and flowers. Darwin guessed that they had all descended from one kind of finch that had somehow made its way from the mainland of South America. Darwin was able to observe the origin of species more closely in the Galapagos than anywhere else, because of the islands' great isolation, which meant there was very little influence from the rest of the world.

Darwin discovered that the Galapagos Islands had animals which were unique although they were related to animals on the South American mainland. Darwin also noticed that there were slight differences between animals of the same species on different islands. It was the governor of the Galapagos Islands who explained to Darwin that he could tell which giant tortoises came from which island by the way the shell was marked and its shape. The reptiles on the Galapagos, for example the two existing species of

(**Above**) *Amidst dramatic scenery, HMS Beagle lies off the coast of Tierra del Fuego.*
(**Right**) *Darwin's name is particularly associated with the Galapagos*

Islands where he made many observations. One of the most striking of these was of the iguana.

land iguana, had grown much larger there than in other places because there were no mammals on the islands to compete with them for food. Indeed, reptiles have become the dominant form of life on some of the islands.

The journey back to England led the *Beagle* to a number of other fascinating places, such as New Zealand where Darwin was intrigued by the elaborate tattoos of the Maoris. With his mind full of all the natural wonders he had seen in South America and the Galapagos he was in a fever to get back to England. Eventually, after a final detour back to South America, rounding

the Cape of Good Hope and completing a round-the-world journey, the *Beagle* arrived back after five years' absence.

It was over twenty years before the theories that first occurred to Darwin on the voyage of the *Beagle* found their way into print. In 1859 his *Origin of Species* was published to an uproar that has still not quite died down, although most people today accept his theory as true.

The voyage of the *Beagle* was possibly one of the most important voyages ever undertaken. It was not only an exploration across the face of the globe, but an exploration into the realm of ideas which was to have a lasting effect on human thought.

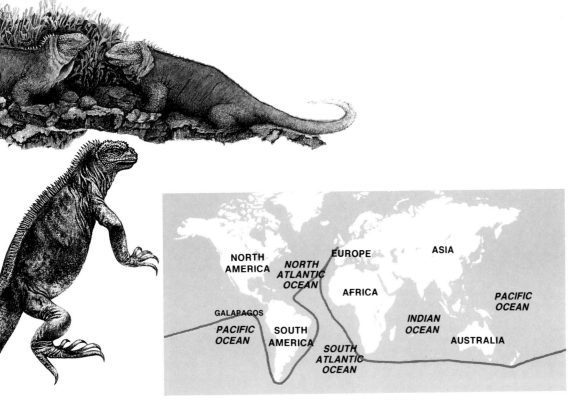

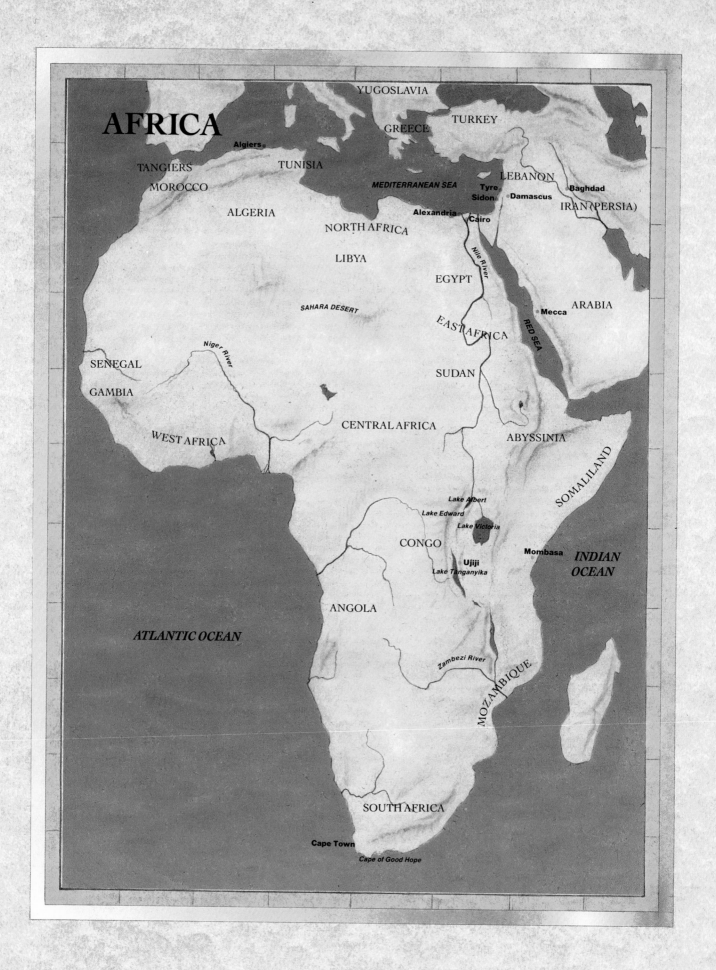

AFRICA

YUGOSLAVIA

GREECE

TURKEY

Algiers

TANGIERS

TUNISIA

LEBANON

MOROCCO

Tyre
Sidon

Damascus

Baghdad

ALGERIA

MEDITERRANEAN SEA

Alexandria

IRAN (PERSIA)

Cairo

NORTH AFRICA

LIBYA

Nile River

EGYPT

ARABIA

SAHARA DESERT

Mecca

EAST AFRICA

RED SEA

SENEGAL

Niger River

GAMBIA

SUDAN

CENTRAL AFRICA

ABYSSINIA

WEST AFRICA

SOMALILAND

Lake Albert

Lake Edward

CONGO

Lake Victoria

Mombasa

INDIAN
OCEAN

Ujiji
Lake Tanganyika

ANGOLA

ATLANTIC OCEAN

Zambezi River

MOZAMBIQUE

SOUTH AFRICA

Cape Town

Cape of Good Hope

(1304–1378)

Muhammed Ibn Abdulla Ibn Battuta was born in Algiers into the family of a judge. His thirty years of travel were to take him on a more extensive journey around the world than even Marco Polo, who was a near contemporary.

After making his way from Tangier across to Alexandria and Cairo, and on to Damascus, from which he travelled across the desert exploring Arabia, he reached Mecca – thus making the pilgrimage so important to Muslims, that of becoming a 'hadji'. From Mecca he travelled on to Baghdad and Shiraz and back to Mecca.

His travels then turned south to explore the Yemen and the eastern coast of Africa. He spent eight years in India and seems to have been well received being feted and treated with great hospitality. He was appointed judge and lived at the court of a cruel Sultan managing to remain in favour except for one occasion when he visited a sheikh whom the Sultan did not like. He only restored himself to the Sultan's good books by relinquishing his property and becoming a hermit. Not only was he reinstated but he was also appointed as an ambassador to go to China.

Travelling with horses, money and ceremonial dresses he set out on further adventures, which included a battle with some rebels and a sojourn in the Maldive Islands and then Ceylon. After leaving Ceylon, however, he was shipwrecked, fell ill with fever, and was robbed by pirates. This occasioned his return to India and the Maldives but he was soon off again to Bengal and Assam where he visited a famous saint who gave him a cloak of goat's hair. A further 40 days from Bengal in a Chinese junk saw him in Java, the Malay peninsula and at last a further month's voyage took him to a calm sea, and China. Some of the stories he brought back from China are scarcely believable.

His most important exploration still lay ahead of him. Ibn Battuta was to cross the Atlas Range of mountains and then the Sahara. This he did with camels by way of Taghaza with its 'houses and mosques built of blocks of salt'.

He eventually reached the Niger, which he refers to as the Nile, and saw that it was flowing to the east, as Mungo Park was to discover some 450 years later.

For eight months he stayed in Mali as a guest of Sultan Sulayman. There were plenty of riches in the court. Gold, silver and crystal were displayed and the slave-girls wore "beautiful robes, and on their heads they have gold and silver fillets, with gold and silver bells attached".

After a stay in Timbuktu, Gao and finally Tagadda, he received a message from the Sultan of Morocco to return to Fez where he settled down.

The Sultan had the foresight to get Ibn Battuta to recount his travels to his secretary which has left us a legacy of knowledge of the Muslim world in the 14th Century, a complement to the descriptions left by Marco Polo.

This detail from a 14th Century map shows Ibn Battuta on one of his journeys (note the camel scourge in his right hand).

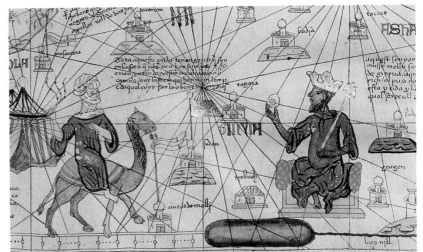

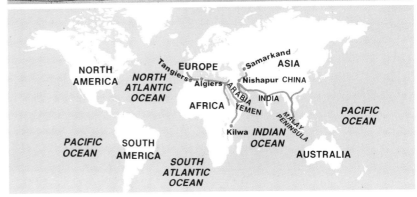

Most of Mungo Park's overland travels were carried out using camels and slaves to transport him and his belongings. He did not have his own slaves but relied on the Slatees – free black merchants who travelled with slaves for the European market. The slaves would look after his needs along the way.

Mungo Park was the first white man to see the Niger River, and though he did not live to reach its mouth he realized the river must eventually flow into the sea – although he believed it first joined the Congo.

A Scotsman from Selkirk, Mungo Park was the seventh of eleven children, and after studying medicine at Edinburgh University he travelled to the East Indies as Assistant Surgeon in 1792 on the recommendation of Sir Joseph Banks, then President of the Royal Society.

Shortly before this an "Association for Promoting the Discovery of the Interior Parts of Africa" had been formed and some three expeditions had set out between 1788 and 1793. At the age of 23 Park left for the Gambia under this African Association which was trying to find out more about the Niger. Both its source and its mouth were a mystery. He was seemingly undaunted by the fact that four explorers had earlier been murdered or died from sickness.

At the British trading post of Pisania, some 200 miles (320 kilometres) inland in the Gambia, Park had an attack of fever, and spent five months recovering and learning the Mandingo language, as well as the local customs of the races who came to trade with the British.

He then set off with an interpreter called Johnson, a young slave, a horse, two asses, a little food, guns, goods to barter, a thermometer, a compass and a pocket sextant.

On his way he was continually beset by natives and relieved of his few possessions. At Fatteconda, in Bondou, the King's harem teased him and "rallied me with a good deal of gaiety upon the whiteness of my skin and the prominency of my nose". He felt very vulnerable when he entered Muslim country. Once in Moorish strongholds, he fell prey to the Ali at Benowm. The Ali had Park brought to him under guard, then imprisoned him as a spy. Three or so months later Park managed to escape on his horse with only his clothes and a compass, and made his way to Segou until he was back in native territory. At last he reached Segou and the "longsought for, majestic Niger, glittering to the morning sun, as broad as the Thames at Westminster, and flowing slowly to the eastward."

He travelled some way along the Niger until the rains broke and he fell ill again. He was attacked by robbers and turned back for Gambia.

At Kamalia he stayed for seven months with a negro, Kaarta Taura, who looked after him while he recovered from the fever. While he was there he watched the way the Mandingo people panned for gold in the dry season. Taura then sent him with his slave caravan back to the coast.

He then sailed for Antigua and the Leeward Islands before he returned to England in December, 1797, two a and half years after leaving. Here he wrote *Travels in the Interior Districts of Africa*, and went back to Peebles where he practised as a surgeon. He married and had a family, but must have found the life tame and managed in 1803 to go again to Africa with the help of Joseph Banks, the African Association and the sponsorship of the Colonial Secretary.

The expedition eventually left in 1805, a party of some 45 Europeans, including soldiers, carpenters and naval boat builders, but it was a badly organized expedition and only eleven of the party ever reached the Niger at Bamaku. This small group proceeded down the river to Sansanding where they remained for two months. Then they made a boat from two canoes. By now there were only five Europeans left, one of whom had gone mad. They sailed 1000 miles (1600 kilometres) southeast down the river hoping to reach the coast. Park had sent his journal and last letters by a messenger and these were the final records of his exploration. In his last letter home he wrote: "Though all the Europeans who are with me should die, and though I myself were half dead, I would still persevere; and if I could not succeed . . . I would at least die on the Niger".

What happened next was never clearly established, but apparently at the Bussa Rapids they were attacked and their boat, the "Joliba" – "the great water" – ran aground. Park and his party jumped into the river where they were drowned, all except for one of the three slaves who had been aboard.

Despite this tragedy this time they had proved that the Niger flowed down towards the Gulf of Guinea, and though Park's journals were lost, the discovery was noted.

Park, who has been described as finely-built, persevering and enterprising was also notable for his humanity and his recognition of the plight of the negroes who were "in a state of hopeless and hereditary slavery, with this aggravation, that their children are born to no other inheritance".

Although Park had not discovered the mouth of the Niger and could prove neither that it was part of the Congo, nor that it flowed into an inland basin, his discoveries were of great value to those who followed him.

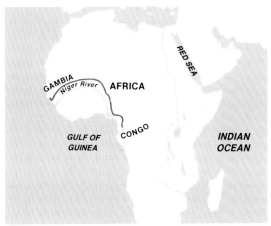

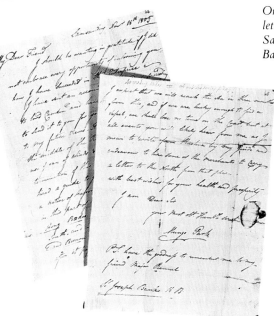

One of Mungo Park's last letters written from Sansanding to Sir Joseph Banks.

Sir Samuel & Florence Baker

(Samuel 1821–1893, Florence – dates not known)

The adventures of Florence and Samuel Baker read like the script for a swash-buckling adventure movie. Baker was a larger-than-life character, a hunter, linguist and administrator and his search for the source of the Nile gave him the opportunity to display his skills at their best. He was to say that pursuing dangerous game was the best training that could be given to an explorer or soldier.

Baker was the son of a wealthy West India shipping merchant and after an early interest in history and geography he spent nine years in Ceylon hunting and adventuring. After his first wife had died of typhus fever he decided to go at his own expense to search for the source of the Nile. With him was Florence, the young Hungarian girl he had reputedly bought in a slave market in the Balkans, and promptly fallen in love with. She was to prove, after her initial timidity, to be a resourceful woman of strong character, adaptable and with a good sense of humour. She was, said Baker, "not a screamer", and was to be his constant loving fellow traveller.

The Bakers arrived in Cairo in March 1861 and spent five months exploring the area around the Atbara, learning Arabic and the use of astronomical instruments.

They must have lived in some comfort – their mansion according to them "comprised entrance hall, dining room, drawing room, lady's boudoir, library, breakfast-room, bedroom and dressing room (with the great advantage of their combination in one circular room fourteen feet (4.3 metres) in diameter)". This hut had white sand for the floor, travelling bedsteads, ornamental Arab baskets and even a dressing table. The Bakers enjoyed travelling in style.

They started their major expedition from Khartoum in 1862, travelling up the Nile with three vessels, 29 transport animals, and a party of 96, including 45 armed men.

At the transit camp of Gondokoro they met Speke and exchanged information. Speke was to explain his discoveries and Baker was to let Speke take his three vessels back down the Nile. They relied on a slave merchant on their way towards the Nile's source, and fell foul of the Bunyoro chief, King Kamrasi. Kamrasi tried to get Baker to leave his wife behind saying "It is my custom to give my visitors pretty wives and I thought you might exchange". A show of arms by Baker made him think twice!

Shortly before they reached Lake Albert, Florence was struck down dramatically with sunstroke, fell into a coma and had to be carried

A watercolour by Sir Samuel Baker, showing him riding a bullock on his journey to Lake Albert.

by litter. Baker was distraught: "Was so terrible a sacrifice to be the result of my selfish exile?"

As the men were preparing a grave for his beloved Florence she recovered and they were able to continue.

Exploration of the Nile

At last, on 14th March, 1864 they reached the lake. "There like a sea of quicksilver, lay far beneath the grand expanse of water – a boundless sea-horizon on the south and southwest, glittering in the noon-day sun; and on the west, at fifty or sixty miles (80 or 96 kilometres) distance, blue mountains rose from the bottom of the lake to a height of about 7,000 feet (2,135 metres) above its level." Sick and weak as they both were, they struggled down to its shores and they named it Lake Albert. They explored the area where the Nile entered the lake, travelling up the river and discovering the dramatic falls they named "Murchison Falls" and seeing also the Albert Nile leaving the lake. Baker was inaccurate in thinking he had found a vast inland sea and it took Stanley (see page 60) to map the area accurately 24 years later.

After further trouble with Kamrasi they joined an Arab caravan and eventually reached Khartoum after two and a half years away. There had been no grand welcome for them at Gondokoro – they had been given up for dead.

While Baker had been away, discussion had mounted concerning the need to curb slave trading and Baker was later appointed Governor-General of the equatorial Nile basin with the missions of suppressing the slave trade and of bringing order to the Sudan. These two things were incompatible given that the slave traders held the key to public order and after various battles Baker realized that few people wanted to get rid of the slave trade.

In 1865, on their return to Europe from Lake Albert Florence and Samuel had married in London but Queen Victoria refused to allow Florence to be presented at court. This was the woman who, with her husband, had been the most intrepid of Victorian explorers – they had been charged by wild beasts, they had survived mutiny and attack by poisoned arrows, been reduced to eating grass, fallen prey to fever, cheated by slave-traders, had their boats

upended by hippopotamuses and in the middle of such horrors the only sign Florence would make to Samuel would be "to touch him quietly on the sleeve".

Another watercolour, again possibly painted by Samuel Baker, showing both Florence and Samuel in a typical African setting.

Richard Burton was the most romantic of all the Victorian Explorers. He was a handsome man of action – as well as a scholar who could speak 35 languages. Disguised as a Pathan, he was one of the few Europeans ever to enter the holy Muslim city of Mecca.

As a young officer in the Indian Army he spent weeks on end living with Muslims and learning about Sufi-ism, a branch of Islam. He was also an expert swordsman and rider.

It is for his search for the source of the River Nile that he is best known. This famous journey has linked his name with that of John Hanning Speke.

On a previous expedition together in Somaliland the two men had been attacked in their camp. A spear had gone through one of Burton's cheeks and out of the other side, and Speke had been wounded in eleven places. The scar shows up clearly in photographs of the older Burton.

This episode did not daunt them and two years later, the pair embarked on the first serious attempt to discover the source of the Nile. In 1856 almost nothing was known about central Africa other than rumours of a great lake at its heart.

They overcame great dangers on their way inland from Zanzibar until they reached Lake Tanganyika. It was Burton's bad luck to have been ill and he stayed behind while Speke went on a journey to the north where he spotted Lake Victoria and guessed it was the true source of the Nile. Burton disagreed and, although he was eventually to be proved wrong, he and Speke fell out over their conflicting claims.

A lifetime of travel and writing followed, as Burton became the British representative in a succession of far-flung places, from each of which he wrote numerous books and articles. This included a period in Damascus which had always been his spiritual home.

After his death his wife destroyed many of his writings. She was a deeply religious lady and probably considered them to be too immoral for publication. Luckily more than enough evidence remains of Burton to reveal what an unconventional and fascinating man he must have been.

Burton dressed as a Pathan. He disguised himself as a Muslim in order to enter the holy city of Mecca.

John Hanning Speke

(1827–1864)

An illustration from one of Richard Burton's books shows the kind of terrain encountered by both Burton and Speke. This is a view in Unyamwezi (the Land of the Moon).

John Speke was no scholar like his fellow explorer, Richard Burton. He was a sportsman, who judged the places he explored by the amount of game there was to hunt.

He saw plenty of active service in the Sikh wars as an Indian Army Officer before joining Burton in an ill-fated expedition into Somaliland. Captured and bound by the Somalis, he charged out of his captors' tent with his hands still tied and spears still whizzing around him. Although he made it to safety he was severely wounded.

On their second expedition Burton contracted malaria before they reached Lake Tanganyika and Speke was almost blind with an eye infection. Speke recovered first and set off alone to search for a larger lake that he knew lay to the north.

A fortnight later, he stood on the shores of a vast lake which he named in honour of Queen Victoria. As far as Speke was concerned he had "solved the problem" but Burton was not so sure.

Later in England, Speke claimed that Lake Victoria was the source of the Nile. This led to an open row with Burton, and the end of their friendship.

Speke had supporters in the Royal Geographical Society, which financed another expedition to confirm his claims. This time he took a friend, James Grant, with him.

Starting out from Zanzibar once more, they travelled between Lake Tanganyika and Lake Victoria. After hospitable treatment from the Kabaka of Buganda, Speke next traced the outlet of the Nile which he identified and named as the Ripon Falls. Due to the presence of unfriendly tribes he was unable to follow the Nile along its entire course into the Sudan through Lake Kyoga and Lake Albert. His enemies took this as an opportunity to belittle his findings.

Back in England, he was about to take part in a debate with Burton in Bath, when accidently or not, he shot himself dead while partridge shooting the night before.

Speke's achievements fell short of his aims, but he opened up a whole area of Africa to European knowledge and paved the way for his friend Samuel Baker to prove the exact route of the Nile after it left Lake Victoria (see page 54).

David Livingstone

(1813–1873)

When David Livingstone first joined the London Missionary Society (LMS) he wanted to go to China, but his destiny lay in Africa. His love for the African people and his condemnation of slavery motivated his exploration.

Born in Blantyre, Scotland, in 1813 he was sent to work in a factory as a "piecer", but from a early age steeped himself in study. He worked from 6 am to 8 pm, went to the factory evening class from 8 pm to 10 pm, then went home and studied till midnight. Eventually at the age of 19, when he was a cotton spinner he had saved enough to attend Greek and medical classes and put himself through college. After joining the LMS, which helped to train him as a doctor, he was sent out to South Africa, to Robert Moffat, whose daughter he later married. He travelled to South Africa via Rio de Janiero, learning some navigation on the way. First in Botswana he learned the habits, laws and customs of local people, built houses and performed various other manual tasks.

He established Christian settlements as he went north, eventually building a mission station in a valley at Kolobeng. There he became friendly with Chief Setshele. At this time he was troubled, not only by lions (one of whom left him with 11 toothwounds and a crushed shoulder which was to trouble him throughout his life), but also by lawless "Boers", Dutch-speaking settlers, who had fled north to escape English law.

In mid-June 1849 Livingstone crossed the Kalahari Desert to reach Lake Ngami, and the following year started off with his wife, Mary, and three children toward King Sebituane, who lived on the north of the lake. As two of his children went down with fever, he returned. Then in June 1851 he discovered the broad Zambezi River, and at the same time was also horrified to see the extent of the slavery, where children had been exchanged for garments.

It was at this stage that Livingstone sent his family home to Britain and spent the next years making his great trans-African journey. It was to be five years before he saw his family again.

When he had left his family at Cape Town he returned to Kolobeng to discover that the Boers had attacked Chief Setshele's land and gutted his own house.

In crossing unknown territory, Livingstone had much use for his sextant.

At the end of 1853 Livingstone set off with a small party of companions to try to reach the west coast of Africa. He and his party all suffered from fever. They had to pay for their food with beads, ornaments and even their clothes. Livingstone had dysentry and at times morale was very low, but Livingstone always put his faith in God and eventually in the middle of 1854 having travelled 1500 miles (2400 kilometres) they reached Luanda. On the return journey he continued to be dogged by illness but once back in the Zambezi Valley from where they had set out, Livingstone decided to travel the river eastwards to its mouth, thus crossing the continent. While some of the party sailed down the Zam-

He returned to England via Bombay, whence he had sailed in the small craft, the *Lady Nyasa*. There he was once more asked to go back to Africa to visit the Rift Valley Lakes and Lake Victoria to find out more about the Nile. He wandered to the west of these lakes, becoming sicker and sicker, obsessed with the idea of finding the Nile among the rivers flowing northwards from central Africa. These last five years were to see him witness to many terrible incidents of slavery.

He reached Ujiji in October 1871 and it was here the historic meeting between Stanley and himself took place. After further illness he died at Ilala. His faithful servants Susi and Chuma, after burying his heart and entrails under a Mupundu tree, embalmed his body and carried it to the coast. Their insistence that he be brought back to England resulted in his burial at Westminster Abbey in 1874.

bezi, others drove the cattle along the banks and Livingstone became the first white man to see the Victoria Falls – Mosi-o-Tunya – the "Smoke That Thunders". He arrived at Quilimane in the middle of 1856 and sailed to Mauritius. He took with him a Makololo headman, who, unnerved by the unfamiliarity of life at sea, went mad and drowned himself.

Once back in England he found himself a popular hero and was appointed to explore east and central Africa. He was equipped with a paddle-steamer call *Ma-Robert*, after his wife (mother of Robert), but beyond Tete they discovered that the Kabora Bassa Rapids could not be navigated. The steamer was also found to be unsuitable, and was nicknamed the "Asthmatic", because of the trouble with her boilers. At this time Livingstone spent much time exploring the Shiré River and eventually Lake Nyasa (Malawi). He was horrified at the slave trade in the area and set up a mission station in the Shiré Highlands. This thwarted expedition – some blame has been laid at Livingstone's door as this essentially lone man lacked the skills to organize larger scale expeditions – was to wind up in 1863. Mary Livingstone, who had joined her husband, had died of the fever and been buried under a large baobab tree.

(*Above*) *Among the items brought back to London after Livingstone's Zambesi expedition were these slave chains.*
(*Centre*) *Ma-Robert, Livingstone's paddle steamer, sailing up the Shiré River.*

Stanley has been described as the explorer who "gathered up the threads, brought together the loose ends, and united the discoveries of his predecessors into one coherent and connected whole". After a terrible childhood he made his way to America. Stanley fought for both sides in the American Civil War and was a soldier and sailor who saw 15 battles, was twice shipwrecked, had travelled widely in the United States, Europe, Asia Minor and to India by the time he was thirty. By this time he was a newspaper correspondent.

He was working on the war in Abyssinia when the *New York Herald* sponsored him to make a search for Livingstone who had been lost some time back.

He left Zanzibar in 1871 and fought his way through flooded rivers, deserting porters, and terrible fever to find Livingstone at Ujiji, on the banks of Lake Tanganyika. He composed himself and coolly "did what cowardice and false pride suggested was the best thing – walked deliberately to him, took off my hat and said:

'Dr Livingstone, I presume?'"

The two very different men became friends. They explored the northern shores of Lake Tanganyika establishing that the river Burton thought flowed out of the lake actually flowed into it.

When Stanley returned to England he received a mixed reception both there and in America. There were suspicions and talk of "humbug".

Nevertheless the *Daily Telegraph* and the *New York Herald* backed a venture for Stanley to complete the, by now, late Livingstone's findings in 1874.

He left from Zanzibar with a boat, the *Lady Alice*, which he had designed and which was carried in sections, and with his numerous porters started on a trip again beset by desertion, fever, food shortage, and attack. Eventually Stanley reached Lake Victoria in February 1875 and circumnavigated it, although not without fighting battles as he went.

Stanley went on to Lake Tanganyika. Livingstone had thought that the Lualaba River, lying to the west of Lake Tanganyika, was part of the Nile River system and Stanley wished to explore the truth of this hope.

Roaring Cataracts

He persuaded the Arab trader, Tippu Tib, to accompany him and they set out with almost 1000 followers, through the dense and steamy jungles, along the river. On one occasion they were attacked by around 2000 warriors but the attackers were always driven back by the party's gunfire. His explorations were all to be tinged with blood and vicious retaliation.

Now the river became the enemy. Stanley encountered seven roaring cataracts round which the men had to carry the heavy boats through the jungle. Swarms of red ants bit and blistered them and worse lay before them. After a quiet widening in the river at what is now called Stanley's Pool a further 32 cataracts lay ahead. Here Stanley's last white companion died and the little mascot boy Kalulu, who had been given to Stanley by an Arab merchant, was swept over a cataract.

At last, after travelling almost 5000 miles (8,000 kilometres) the gloomy and rebellious little group neared the sea. By the time they were back in Zanzibar only 82 of the original party of 359 were left.

Stanley was to embark on one more historic mission – that of rescuing the governor of Equatoria, Emin Pasha – who had been isolated when the Sudan was evacuated after the death of Gordon of Khartoum.

Having raised £20,000 Stanley's expedition set out in March 1887 from the mouth of the Congo, and comprised over 800 people, some of them Tippu Tib's wives. He planned to leave the river then cross to Lake Albert to Emin Pasha's headquarters. Crossing "the Great Forest" put them through terrible ordeals of snakes, hunger, aggressive primitive tribesmen and took them through the gloomy, steamy, dank, rain forest.

When they did arrive, the Pasha, who was in good health and well dressed, did not seem at all anxious to leave.

After a further trip to find his following party Stanley remonstrated with the Pasha and together they eventually made their way to Zanzibar with some 1500 people. Most of them disappeared en route and only three-quarters of Stanley's original expedition returned with him.

On this trip Stanley had seen also the Ruwenzori "Mountains of the Moon" and discovered Lake Edward, but he was to remain a controversial, often misunderstood figure with a reputation for being "readier to shoot natives than negotiate with them".

STANLEY EXPEDITION.

MEETING OF EMIN PASHA AND M⁽ᴿ⁾ STANLEY, AT KAVALLI, April 29⁽ᵗʰ⁾ 1888.

*(**Above**) Stanley's last mission was to "rescue" Emin Pasha.*
*(**Below**) Stanley's boots and hat used at some time during his African explorations.*

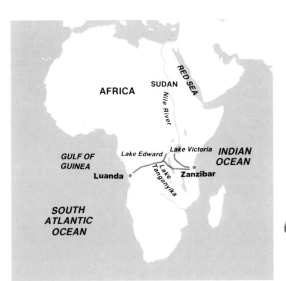

Mary Kingsley is known not only as a traveller and explorer who went "alone without protection among cannibals and with cannibals" in an age that still believed in chaperones for women, but also as someone who did much to help change attitudes towards the Africans.

In the eight years of her working life, four of which were in the public eye, she showed a great spirit of adventure, a compassion for the people among whom she travelled and a strong belief in justice.

She was born in London where she spent her childhood and youth before going about her womanly duties with dedication and a belief in that role. She received no official education barring the study of German, but she read voraciously. She had access to a fine library of books from her adventurer-writer father. Her father travelled widely and she saw no fault in his leaving his family, even though the toll on her mother's life was great.

At 17 she was described as a "thin pale girl of middle height, with straight fair hair and blue eyes, quiet and of domestic habits", but when the family moved to Cambridge where her

brother was staying she gained confidence in the company of worldly men and women, and in 1888 went to Paris for a week with a friend. This was the only travelling she had done before she set off for the Canaries following the death of her parents within weeks of each other. Now at 30 years old, having nursed and cared for her family she had no responsibility, no one to depend on her and her trip to the Canaries opened her eyes to all sorts of possibilities.

Deciding against the study of medicine which had been her intention, she determined to carry on with work that her father had not completed on native religion and law. She had been helping her father in his work and through self-education had a wide knowledge of many subjects – including mechanics and electricity as well as anthropology.

Still mourning for her parents she said of her first trip to West Africa that she went there to die, but "West Africa amused me and was kind to me and was scientifically interesting – and did not want to kill me just then". She was encouraged to collect beetles and freshwater fishes, and on her trip on a cargo boat she increased her already extensive knowledge of seamanship and piloting. She travelled through swamp, bush and on river, and by the time she returned to England she had learned some of the customs and religion of the Fjort tribe in the Congo.

She attracted enough attention with her specimens for the British Museum to provide her with a collector's outfit, and she lost little time in preparing for another expedition. She sailed again in December 1894, touching at West African ports and spending two months at Old Calabar. She then went southwards to the French Congo, and despite attempts made to dissuade her, went up the dangerous Ogowé River. When it was pointed out that she was unaccompanied, she replied that "neither the Royal Geographical Society's list, nor any other, of articles necessary to travellers in tropical climates, makes mention of husbands". She travelled with no other Europeans and was met and was entertained by cannibals.

At Efoua where she was given a native hut to sleep in she noticed a strange smell, and opening a bag discovered "a human hand, three big toes, four eyes, two ears, and other human bits". She

(***Above & Below***) *Fjort natives of Kacongo and*   *Loango in European dress outside trading stores.*

quickly replaced them and no doubt the sense of humour for which she became well-known, and her strong stomach, allowed her to view her experience with equanimity.

She travelled always as a trader, paying her way trading with rubber and oil, and she said of the traders that they knew Africa better than all the other sorts of white men put together.

While on her travels, she climbed the Mungo Mah Lobeh Mountain, 13,760 feet (4,194 metres) high, ate snake, ran into elephants and gorillas, and was once saved from death by her heavy Victorian skirt when she fell 15 feet (4.6 metres) onto spikes in a game pit.

When she returned in November 1895, she wrote "Travels in West Africa" and her humour and knowledge made her a popular speaker and writer. She championed the cause of the African, pointing out that to govern wisely in Africa it was necessary to understand the African mind, and that native laws and customs needed to be "harmonized" with those of the English administration.

She had an attractive personality and as well as her sense of humour her conversation was brilliant, but her health suffered under the strain of work in London, and she sailed to Cape Town in 1900. It was during the Boer War and she offered her services, which were accepted at the Simons Town Palace Hospital, where she nursed Boer prisoners of war.

She helped convert the chaos she found there into order, but in her zeal she caught enteric fever, and after an operation died of heart failure. She had asked that if it should not be possible to send her body back to England she could be buried at sea. This she was and was given a funeral with full naval and military honours. She had not even reached her thirty-eighth birthday.

A Calabar chief. All the pictures of Africans seen here are from Mary Kingsley's own book. They show very little of the real way of African life and show instead the way in which books of the time liked to present the natives — dressed in European clothes in poses reminiscent of old Victorian photographs.

(*Above*) *Freya Stark in Arab dress. She chose to travel in such clothes as they were comfortable and more practical for desert travel.*

(*Right*) *The countries she travelled in were mainly of rough, desert terrain such as this.*

Traveller, writer, geographer, historian and archaeologist, Dame Freya Stark was born in Paris in 1893 a daughter of artistic parents.

By the age of 13 she was widely read, could speak perfect Italian and could read French and was teaching herself Latin. When she was 14 she had an accident in a factory she was visiting. Her scalp was badly torn when her long hair caught up in a steel shaft and dragged her round. She spent four months in hospital having skin grafts but would always be sensitive about her appearance. The ordeal however, helped to give her the great courage and mental stamina she later needed to face the demands she placed on herself.

In the First World War she trained as a nurse but caught typhoid which was complicated by pleurisy, then pneumonia. At one time her temperature rose to 107°F. Throughout her life she would be beset by illness but this never tied her down for long. As well as nursing, Freya worked in the Censor's office reading French, German and Italian letters. After the war she helped run her mother's home in Italy but fell ill again. In the winter of 1924 she had an operation for a gastric ulcer and while she recuperated she learnt 17th Century embroidery, and Arabic. She decided at this time that "the most interesting things in the world were likely to happen in

the neighbourhood of oil" and after the tragic death of her sister, Vera, she set off in November 1927 for Beirut.

In Brummana in the Lebanon she practised her Arabic, did a great deal of walking and fell in love with the East, in particular the desert: "I never imagined that my first sight of the desert would come as such a shock of beauty and enslave me right away". She spent seven months in the East before returning to Europe but in Autumn 1929 she was off again, this time to Baghdad, by way of Bombay and the Persian Gulf.

At that time Baghdad had primitive lighting and sanitation but a romantic history and British connections that appealed to her. Freya preferred to wear Arab clothes and she disdained the colonial lifestyle. She lived modestly with a shoemaker's family in a simple room, and she started to learn Persian.

She made trips in to Luristan in 1930 and 1931. High in the mountains she collapsed with dysentery, then malaria, and when she reached Teheran she learned that her father had died. When she returned to Baghdad she was offered a job writing for the *Baghdad Times*.

By the time Freya returned to London in 1933 she was a well-known figure. She was not so much an explorer braving unknown country, but a traveller; her presentation of Arabia with all its colour and dignity brought a fresh perspective of the East.

Dogged by Illness

She was off again in January 1935 armed with cameras and instruments and bound for Shabwa in the Hadhramaut, South Arabia. She travelled by donkey through stony desert and visited harems, but measles and then dysentery led to a mercy flight by an RAF bomber taking Freya on a stretcher to Aden Hospital.

Freya then attempted a "dig" with an archeologist to try to find if there had been any cultural contact between Arabia and Africa in Roman times at Hadhramaut, but the personalities of the two women were incompatible and they broke up the party. Freya went on alone to Husn-el-Ghurab to try to establish whether it was Cana the city of Biblical times. Her detailed and careful descriptions brought her credit. She also travelled to see crusader castles and her fearlessness stood her in good stead when she reduced a would-be-robber to kissing her hand after he had unwisely tried to rob her.

In April 1941 Freya was one of the last people to get into Baghdad when four Iraqui colonels had seized power and closed its gates. The British Embassy was besieged and true to their image, the way of life remained throughout this dangerous time, the British continuing to serve drinks on the lawn, exercise their polo ponies and generally "keep up standards"! At the end of May the colonels were driven off.

In June 1942 the Royal Geographical Society presented Freya with its Founders Medal. She went on to lecture in America, then to India where she travelled and talked. By the time the war ended she was a public figure, highly thought of in the Arab world. She married in 1947 but the marriage did not last.

She revelled in youthful company and has never stopped travelling despite the ill health which continued to plague her. At the age of 76 she went camping at 9,000 feet (2,740 metres) in the Himalayas and was back again ponytrekking around Annapurna ten years later.

In 1972 she was made a Dame of the British Empire and she lives in Asolo in Italy, which she has known since childhood.

The most common way of travelling was by camel and Freya Stark became adept at using the camel for transport.

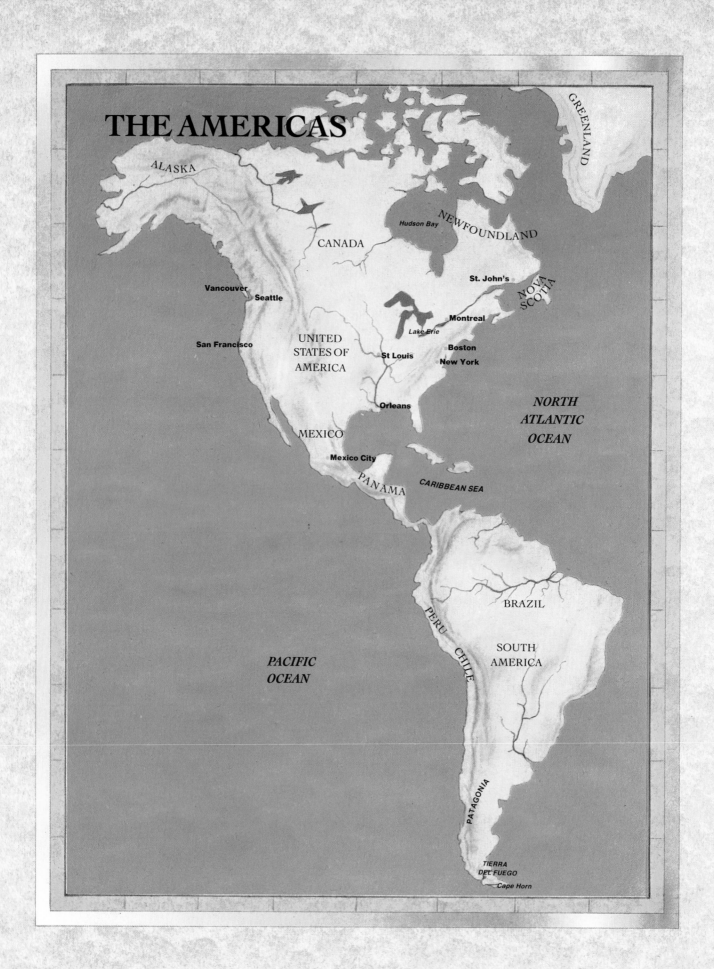

THE AMERICAS

GREENLAND

ALASKA

NEWFOUNDLAND

Hudson Bay

CANADA

St. John's

NOVA SCOTIA

Vancouver

Seattle

Montreal

Lake Erie

San Francisco

UNITED STATES OF AMERICA

St Louis

Boston

New York

NORTH ATLANTIC OCEAN

Orleans

MEXICO

Mexico City

PANAMA

CARIBBEAN SEA

BRAZIL

PERU

CHILE

SOUTH AMERICA

PACIFIC OCEAN

PATAGONIA

TIERRA DEL FUEGO

Cape Horn

When the first European explorers crossed the isthmus of Panama to the Pacific Ocean under Bilboa, one of their expedition was the illegitimate son of a poor officer in the Spanish Army, a man unable to read or write, who had earlier earned his living as a swineherd. This was in the early 1500s and rumours reached the expedition in Panama of the vast golden empire that lay to the south.

Fired by thoughts of gold Pizarro and a companion, Almagro, borrowed the money to venture on an exploration of the west coast of South America. They reached as far as the edges of the Inca Empire. Two expeditions then sent from Panama failed to conquer the kingdom and Pizarro sought aid from Spain. He was made governor of Peru, before he had even conquered it – no doubt the gold, silver and vicuna skins he had brought back were enough to make the Spaniards have faith in his venture.

In May 1532 Pizarro landed with his party in South America and making their way over the treacherous peaks of the Andes with 62 horsemen, 106 infantry, 20 crossbows and three muskets, they made for the headquarters of the Inca chief.

They were fortunate at that time that the empire was in the throes of civil war and their leader, a usurper, named Atahualpa, a "ruthless and vengeful" man, favoured the adventurers and had used the efficient postinghouse system to tell his people not to harm the pale-skinned yellow-haired strangers. He no doubt felt secure that once in his land they would be at his mercy.

They reached Cajamarca where Atahualpa and his army of 50,000 gave the town over to the strangers. When Pizarro invited Atahualpa in he was carried in on a litter by 80 chiefs dressed in gold and silver and accompanied by four to five thousand soldiers. The treacherous Spanish tried to make him recognize their God and their sovereignty but Atahualpa, son of the Sun God threw their book, which he undoubtedly did not understand, to the ground. Pizarro gave the order for his men to fight through the "wall of living flesh" to get at Atahualpa and they took him prisoner.

Atahualpa offered a room full of gold and two of silver as ransom but the treacherous Spanish let Atahualpa's people collect the gold together

and hand it over before they tried him for offences such as plotting against them. He was sentenced to death. At first the execution was to be by fire but when he consented to be baptized they allowed Atahualpa death by strangulation. The conquest and plunder went on and Pizarro eventually founded a new capital at Lima. Despite the Inca revolt against the greed and cruelty of the Spanish it was Pizarro's own people who killed him. His partner, Almagro, quarrelled with Pizarro over the division of spoils and in the following civil war Almagro was beheaded. His followers rose against Pizarro and murdered him in 1541 and he died making a cross of his own blood on the ground crying to his God for mercy. He had done much evil in his acclaimed mission to save souls. He had conquered a great empire and destroyed it utterly.

Riches such as this solid gold Llama attracted Pizarro to South America.

NORTH ATLANTIC OCEAN

PANAMA

Cajamarca

Lima PERU SOUTH AMERICA

INCA EMPIRE

PACIFIC OCEAN

Hernando Cortés

(1485–1547)

Cortez holds his sword high in a gesture of encouragement to his men as the siege of the city of Tenochtitlan finally ends and they take it by storm.

Hernando Cortés has been called the "greatest of the conquistadores" and certainly he was absolutely fearless, mercilessly cruel and firmly believed that it was his mission to convert the heathen to Christianity and stop human sacrifice and cannibalism. The fact that he was also greedy for gold and wealth does not seem to have been at odds with his convictions.

Cortés was born into a noble family in western Spain. A man of culture and social standing, he studied law and at the age of 19 emigrated to Hispaniola where he became a lawyer and farmer. In 1511 he sailed with Diego Velazquez to conquer Cuba and helped to administer the colony. He had already made his ambitions clear: "I come to get gold, not to till the soil like a peasant".

Velazquez appointed him leader of an expedition to explore Yucatan and establish a colony on the mainland, a decision he was later to regret when Cortés refused his orders and established himself as governor there.

Cortés landed at Tabasco in 1519 and gave orders that his ships be burned. The only way to go was onward. After a battle with the local natives he learned of the great Aztec Empire further inland. He took three months to cross the 200 miles (320 kilometres) of mountain passes with its savage tribes, and news of the white-faced, black-haired, bearded strangers with magic firearms reached the Aztec King, Montezuma, in his beautiful capital Tenochtitlan (where Mexico City now stands) on its island in a lake.

The king, while he distrusted the strangers, accepted them with friendliness, hospitality, and gifts of gold. He believed Cortés might be the reincarnation of the Aztec God, Quetzalcoatl. Despite Cortés' speech of friendship, the Spaniards soon took the king captive, forcing him to act as their puppet and to order his subjects to collect gold. When Montezuma's brother led a rebellion against the Spaniards, Montezuma was stoned, and refusing any treatment, he died. The Spaniards had to fight their way out of the capital by night along the narrow causeways connecting it to the mainland.

After his escape, Cortés returned to lay siege to the Aztecs. Many of them had already died in a smallpox epidemic probably brought by the Spaniards, but for three months they held out. The water around the city became "red with the blood of the dead and dying".

When Cortés entered the city he destroyed it utterly – more than 240,000 Aztecs perished, and within a few years every vestige of the Aztec civilization had been obliterated.

Cortés made further expeditions but was largely unsuccessful and he made many enemies. In 1540 he returned to Spain where he later died deeply in debt, a sad and disillusioned man. The gold for which he and his comrades "longed and lusted for", for which they had "hungered like pigs" had brought him no lasting happiness and he had wiped out a magnificent empire, through guile and treachery, in the name of Christianity.

NORTH AMERICA

Mexico City

CUBA

Tabasco

HISPANIOLA

PACIFIC OCEAN

(c.1755–1820)

Alexander Mackenzie was a Scottish fur trader who became the first European to cross the Rockies.

As a young man he emigrated to Canada and worked for a fur-trading company and, later, at a trading post in northern Alberta.

With a small party of Canadians and Indians he set out in June 1789 to try to find out whether the major river from the Great Slave Lake flowed into the Arctic or the Pacific. The group travelled in birch bark canoes down the Slave River to the Great Slave Lake. Although it was summer the weather was very cold, and only the courage and perseverance of the group under Mackenzie's skilled leadership, drove them on. The ice on the lake was unstable, but they managed to cross it and found a wide, rapidly flowing river to the west. They followed it for more than 1000 miles (1,600 kilometres) and were disappointed to discover it took them into the Arctic Ocean.

After this exploration of the Mackenzie River, Mackenzie spent time improving his knowledge of surveying, navigation, and nautical astronomy and was soon ready for another venture.

This time he set out to look for a route to the Pacific by following the Peace River which flowed into Athabasca from the west. The party left Fort Chipewyan in 1792 and after wintering up the Peace River they started off towards the Rockies in May 1793 hoping that they would reach the headwaters and find a navigable river, over the ridge, on the other side. Imagine their dismay to discover not one ridge when they reached the divide, but a series of mountains and crags stretching many miles.

Eventually, after struggling over the top and finding a narrow, fast-flowing waterway they made their way downstream, at one time damaging their canoe when they hit a sandbank and losing most of their stores and ammunition. They patched it up and swept down the Fraser. The Indians were so impressed by Mackenzie's bravery that they accepted him and helped him. They told him of the Fraser's rapids and canyons so Mackenzie and his party hid their canoe and went on foot, braving their way through hail, snow and forest. Eventually they met some more Indians who fed them and told them of a

river which led to salt water. The Indians lent them canoes and they soon reached a narrow inlet filled with seagulls, seals and porpoises. They had reached the Pacific but because the Indians on the coast were threatening they made haste to return to their friends upstream.

The going was easy as they travelled back the way they had come and on August 23rd they triumphantly entered Fort Chipewyan firing their rifles and waving their flags. 1.500 miles (2,400 kilometres) back, the Pacific coast behind them, Mackenzie had left an inscription on a stone, seen here in the illustration.

*When he finally reached the Pacific Coast Mackenzie left this rough but lasting record (**below**) of his achievement. It is known as Mackenzie's Rock.*

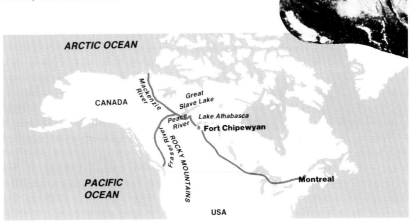

=== *Alexander von Humboldt* ===

(1769–1859)

Humboldt and Bonpland in their jungle hut. Notice the large array of navigational instruments and the variety of botanical specimens.

Alexander von Humboldt is best known for two scientific discoveries: he identified the cause of mountain sickness and he calculated the effect of altitude on temperature. These discoveries were not made by Humboldt in any laboratory, and the path that led him to them was a fascinating and dangerous one.

Born in Berlin in 1769 the son of a Prussian army major, Humboldt showed an early interest in science and by the age of twenty knew that he wanted to be an explorer. To this end he studied biology, geology, astronomy, botany and languages.

In 1797 after spending some years working for the Prussian government in the mining department he tried to join an organized expedition but because of the Napoleonic Wars he was

unable to do so. So he approached the Spanish government himself and got permission to visit the Spanish colonies in Central and South America, at his own expense.

With the French botanist Aimé Bonpland he spent the five years from 1799 to 1804 travelling more than 6000 miles (9,600 kilometres) in the colonies – on foot, by canoe and on horseback.

They travelled across dusty plains and sailed on the Orinoco River looking for a link between the Orinoco and Amazon River water systems. They came upon the Amazon's magnificent tributary the Rio Negro River, where 1200 miles (1,920 kilometres) inland they saw freshwater dolphins. They found the river link between the Orinoco and the Rio Negro branch of the Amazon and on the way collected some 12,000 botanical specimens.

They made their way through dense tropical forest in humid heat, beset by mosquitoes. Their food supplies ran short and they lived on wild cacao beans and river water. Their reports contained horrifying descriptions of entering Indian huts where they saw the revolting remnants of meals of human flesh.

Another trip saw them in the Andes and they travelled along what is now the Pan American highway over the steep rocky paths and climbed the volcanoes Quito, Ecuador and Chimborazo.

They both suffered from mountain sickness and Humboldt realized it was due to lack of oxygen, an important discovery that would aid climbers from then on. He also calculated that the temperature dropped $1°F$ for every 300 feet of height.

Among other scientific investigations he studied the currents off the west coast of America, and the Humboldt Current is named after him.

From 1804 to 1827 he lived in Paris publishing his discoveries and meeting scientists. Then he returned to Berlin exhausted and impoverished where he became tutor to the German Crown Prince. He helped to make science more understandable and interesting for the ordinary man and finally published his work *Kosmos*. He died in his 90th year.

(Above) An illustration drawn by Humboldt showing the type of bridge built by the local people which often linked causeways high up in the mountains or were built across rivers.
(Left) Often they would moor the boats by the banks of the river to make a riverside camp.

═══ *Meriwether Lewis & William Clark* ═══

(Lewis 1744–1809, Clark 1770–1838)

(Top) William Clark and (below) Meriwether Lewis.
(Right) The falls of the Peloos River.

When Napoleon sold the French Louisiana Territory to the United States in 1803 for 15 million dollars President Jefferson lost no time in urging an exploration across the continent. He appointed his secretary, Meriwether Lewis, a frontiersman and soldier, and his army companion William Clark to undertake the expedition.

Their brief was to explore the upper Missouri to find a water route so that trade to the Pacific could be opened up, to chart and map the area, to make contact with the Indians and to examine the flora, fauna and soil.

After wintering at St Louis a party of some 40 men set out with three boats, one of them a keelboat which could be sailed, rowed, poled or towed, carrying 21 bales of goods for trading, and two small wooden boats, called pirogues.

They wintered 1,600 miles (2,560 kilometres) up the Missouri at Fort Mandan where they celebrated Christmas and where their interpreter and his Indian wife, Sacagawea, had a child. They sent their keelboat back and made six dugouts to supplement their pirogues.

In April 1804 they headed upstream naming rivers as they went and reaching the source of the Missouri. They reached the Rocky Mountains in August, thinking that a short trek would take them over the mountains to the Columbia headwaters. They had not met the Indians whom they had hoped to get horses from and the men were tired after hauling the boats against the strong stream. Just over what is now Lemhi Pass they met Sacagawea's tribesmen, the Shoshoni, and were able to buy horses and get information. There was no hunting here and the men ate what they could find surrounded by snow, even in September. They reached the River Clearwater, built new canoes and first sailed down the Clearwater, then the River Snake and River Columbia. They had to carry their boats round the Cascades, in one case making an 18 mile (29 kilometres) detour. By the time they reached the Pacific they had faced sickness, hunger, rattlesnakes and grizzly bears. One grizzly chased six hunters out of the forest despite eight bullet wounds.

In March 1806 they made their way back, Clark following the Yellowstone River, Lewis, the Marias River, and made a triumphant entry into St Louis at the end of September firing their guns as a salute to the town.

They had travelled over 7000 miles (11,200 kilometres) in two and a half years and opened the route across America. It was mainly because of their findings that the US based its claims to the territories which later became known as Oregon and Washington.

Clark become Superintendent of Indian affairs but Lewis had a strange and tragic end when, in 1809, strangely clothed and talking to himself, he arrived at a cabin in Chickasaw country where he later shot himself.

THE POLAR REGIONS

USA

Victoria Strait

Lancaster Sound

NORTH POLE

RUSSIA

NORWAY

AFRICA

SOUTH AMERICA

SOUTH POLE

Mt. Erebus

Bay of Whales

AUSTRALIA

James Weddell
(1787–1834)

Many explorers owe their fame to a combination of skill and luck, but for James Weddell luck seems to have played an even greater part than usual in allowing him to set a record for navigation in the Antarctic.

Weddell was the son of an upholsterer who died young, leaving a widow and two young children. The young Weddell received very little education although he made the most of what he had and read whatever he could. He began his career in the merchant service and then transferred to the Royal Navy. He became a midshipman and an excellent navigator. Later he was to be described by an Admiral of the Fleet as "one of the most efficient and trustworthy officers that I have met with in the course of my professional life."

After leaving the navy Weddell took command of the brig *Jane* and became a seal hunter although he could not have had much experience in this field.

After his first voyage to the Antarctic in 1819 he was able to buy a share in *Jane* and after being away two years he soon set off again on a second trip. He visited South Georgia, the South Shetlands and South Orkneys in 1821 and 1822, exploring and navigating and searching for the fur-seals of his trade.

On his third voyage, which began in 1822, he surveyed the South Shetlands and South Orkneys and then headed south in search of other new lands. Although he was a fisherman he has been described as "having the heart of an explorer" and this curiosity and his excellent skill as a navigator urged him into a severe and normally impenetratable region as far as 74°15′S. This was further than Captain Cook's record by more than 3° and would remain a record until James Clark Ross, using Weddell's log book, broke it in 1842. Weddell had been able to venture this far only because the seas were unusually free of ice – the sea was still and "perfectly clear of field ice" said Weddell. It was late in the season and the approaching winter wisely decided Weddell to return using the south blowing wind.

He named the sea the "Sea of George IV" but it is now the Weddell Sea, named after this remarkable navigator whose longitude calculations were of amazing accuracy. He was not a scientist and yet he took back to London some unique specimens of sea leopard; he noted every day the temperatures of air and water and the variations of the compass, and less scientifically, after giving his crew a double ration of rum, he threw a bottle with a message into the sea.

On his way home Weddell climbed a peak in South Georgia and was amazed to see that the mercury in one of his instruments, showing the artificial horizon, was trembling – he was recording volcanic quavers.

On his return in 1824 Weddell published a good account of his discoveries in *A Voyage Towards the South Pole*. It would be nearly a hundred years before the full voyage was made.

James Weddell died unmarried at the age of 47 in London.

(Right) This picture of a "Sea Leopard" was drawn by Weddell and shows a much fiercer creature than perhaps was the case!

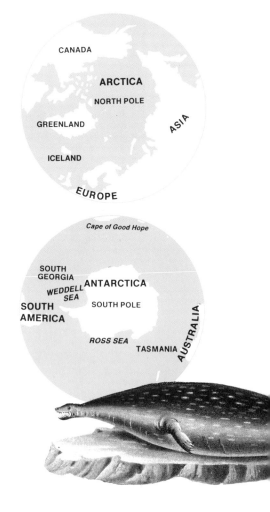

John Ross little knew when he commanded the ship *Isabella* on an expedition to find the North West Passage in the Arctic, that one day that very ship would save him and his nephew after they had spent four continuous winters in the Arctic.

That first trip was in 1818 and on the voyage John Ross thought he saw mountains he called "Croker Mountains" across the neck of Lancaster Sound.

When Edward Parry and Ross's nephew James Clark, later found that there were no Croker Mountains, John Ross was for a time discredited.

The Admiralty wouldn't sponsor a further expedition to continue his search for a North West Passage but when a gin distiller, Felix Booth, put up the money, John and his nephew, James Clark set off in *Victory* and eventually reached what they named Boothia, in the Canadian Arctic. They set up winter quarters here with the help of the Eskimo, who provided dog teams.

James Clark made a number of important expeditions using sledges. He discovered the magnetic pole at 70°5′N, 96°46′W and crossed the isthmus of Boothia. He also crossed King William's Island which he thought was part of the mainland. This mistake was later to cost an expedition under Sir John Franklin dear. Had they known it was an island he might have chosen the sheltered path to the south of it, which would possibly have been navigable. The loss of some of his 134 men might have been averted and they might have found the North-West passage they sought.

Unable to release the ships from the ice, John Ross's party made their way to Lancaster Sound – they were helped on their expedition by using supplies from *Fury*, a ship that had previously

been abandoned by another exploration party. At the Sound they were rescued by the *Isabella,* and returned to England where John Ross was knighted in 1834. His triumph in bringing back all but three of his men after four winters in the Arctic vindicated his earlier mistake.

In 1839 James Clark Ross was appointed to command an expedition to set up magnetic observatories at St. Helena, Cape of Good Hope, Kerguelen Island and Tasmania and to explore the Antarctic. He and Captain Crozier sailed with two ships, the *Erebus* and the *Terror* which had been strengthened to resists ice pressure. In January 1841 he crossed the Antarctic Circle and he steered into a large sea now named the Ross Sea. They saw vast snowclad mountains and two great volcanos they called Erebus and Terror, and reached a latitude of 78°4′S. Ross followed the great southern ice barrier for 250 miles (400 kilometres).

He made three attempts to go beyond the pack ice. In the four years he was away he lost only one man through illness and he too was knighted, in 1843.

Later both Rosses separately tried to find Franklin when his expedition was lost in the Arctic, without achieving any success. James Clark's friend, Captain Crozier, from the Antarctic expedition was among those lost.

(**Top**) *Sir James Clark Ross* and (**below**) *Sir John Ross.*
(**Above**) *James Clark Ross painted this water colour impression of the coast of Antarctica in 1841. In the foreground is Ross's ship HMS Erebus and in the distance is Mount Erebus, the volcano named after the ship.*

Fridtjof Nansen
(1861–1930)

Fridtjof Nansen was not only a great explorer, oceanographer and scientist but also a statesman and humanist who was awarded the Nobel Prize for Peace in 1922.

Born in Norway near Christiana, now Oslo, in 1861, he studied zoology at university and as a young man had a great love for the outdoors. A fine athlete, skater, skier, hunter and fisherman, his physique developed to give him the stamina and endurance he would need for the trials ahead.

After joining a sealing trip in the Greenland waters he devised a plan to cross Greenland on skis, and with a party of six the expedition started in 1888 from the uninhabited east coast of the island. They left in August, knowing that the only way to go was forward and headed in a northwest direction. Hauling the sledges uphill was difficult work, especially since the storms and bitter cold added to the dangers of breaking through snow-bridges and negotiating crevasses.

They reached the highest point of almost 9000 feet (2,740 metres) in early September and made for the west coast where after 40 days they arrived. They had to spend the winter in Greenland and Nansen spent his time studying the Eskimo. He returned to Norway in May 1889.

He then dreamed up a scheme that was called by an American "an illogical scheme of self-destruction". He wanted to build a special boat that would not be crushed by ice but that would rise up on to it, and would drift from a chosen destination to the North Pole.

He presented the idea to both the Norwegian Geographical Society and the Royal Geographical society and in 1893, despite criticisms of the scheme, and partly backed by the Norwegian parliament, the *Fram* ("Forward") set off with 13 men.

North of the New Siberian Islands the *Fram* became enclosed by ice and stood up well to the pressure. The party had dogs, sledges, kayaks and the Norwegian flag. Their clothing was much lighter than the usual skins and furs and they had electricity supplied by a wind-driven dynamo. Although the *Fram* drifted for two years she did not reach the Pole and in 1895, leaving *Fram* at 84°4′N, 102°27′E some 350 miles (560 kilometres) south of the Pole Nansen went off with dogsleds, kayaks and one companion.

(Right) The beautiful colours of the Northern Lights inspired Nansen to make this chalk drawing.

Their progress was slow because of the huge ridges of ice. Then the spring thaw forced them back but they had reached 86°14′N, the highest latitudes yet achieved by man.

In August they reached the open sea. Sadly they had to shoot the last two dogs that had so faithfully worked with them but there was no room for them on the kayaks that they lashed together. They took 11 months to reach safety

lems and his knowledge of when to take risks must have been as valuable to him as a statesman as they were to him as an explorer.

He was an impressive man, tall and thin and, in later years, with snow-white hair and a flowing moustache. In 1930 he wanted to fly over the North Pole to celebrate his birthday but he died before he was able to do this.

and had to spend a winter on an island from late August 1895 to mid May 1896. They built a hut of stone covered with walrus hides and lived on polar bear and walrus meat, using blubber as fuel. On one occasion they nearly lost their kayaks when they came adrift and Nansen bravely hurled himself into the icy waters to retrieve them. On another occasion a large bull-walrus attacked Nansen's canoe, nearly destroying it.

Making their way toward Spitzbergen they were lucky enough to meet Frederick Jackson, whose name was given to the island on which Nansen and his companion stayed. They returned to Norway on Jackson's ship after nearly three years away. They arrived at Christiana on September 9th and the *Fram* arrived soon after them. It had drifted around but not over the Pole and had returned safely. The voyage had proved that the North Pole was a deep ice-covered sea.

Nansen went on to pursue other scientific interests, particularly oceanography, until 1917.

As he grew older he became more involved in politics and in 1920 he headed the Norwegian delegation at the first assembly of the United Nations, receiving the Nobel Peace prize in 1922 for his work in organizing relief for the victims of the terrible Russian famine. His thorough planning, careful evaluation of possible prob-

(Below) Nansen's boat made by lashing together two kayaks.

Roald Amundsen

(1872–1928)

(Below) Two of the Fram crew members with their meteorological observatory. They took readings every four hours.

From the time he was a teenager Roald Amundsen knew he wanted to be a Polar explorer.

Born into a family of seamen and shipowners he was to achieve fame not only for sailing the North West Passage – a route that had escaped explorers for hundreds of years – but also as being the first man to reach the South Pole.

Amundsen first studied medicine before sailing with a Belgian expedition in 1897. It was the first expedition to spend the winter in the Antarctic.

In the summer of 1903 Amundsen, backed by Nansen (see page 76), took the *Gjoa* to the Arctic where two winters were spent on King William's Island. In 1904 they carried out scientific work and befriended the Eskimo and learnt much about living in the Arctic. In August 1905 they braved the ice floes in Victoria Strait and sailed through the up-to-now unsolved link across the north of the American continent. The party spent another winter off the mouth of the Mackenzie River, returning in 1906.

When Amundsen was planning to reach the North Pole, Nansen had let him take the *Fram* but when he heard that an American, Peary, had beaten him to it in 1909 Amundsen did an about-face. In 1910 he sailed for Madeira and there told his crew that they would be going south instead. Among the sealed instructions he left to be opened a few days after they left was a request to send a telegram to Robert Falcon Scott (see page 80) who was preparing to try for the South Pole: "Beg leave," it went, "inform you proceeding Antarctic – Amundsen". Scott received it late in 1910.

Once in the Antarctic, Amundsen made his base camp at the Bay of Whales, some 60 miles (96 kilometres) nearer to the Pole than Scott's but on the ice shelf itself. The party established depots, the furthest being 82°S, and then they set off on October 19th 1911 – Amundsen, four companions and four sledges each drawn by 13 dogs. His full party had been eight men and 118 dogs; Scott had had 33 dogs and 19 ponies.

From latitude 85°S they started on their final leg. On November 17th they passed mountains with peaks rising to 15,000 feet (4,570 metres) and had good weather until a blizzard stopped them for five days. Despite agonizing frost sores in temperatures of −43°C (−44°F) and the dangers of crevassed ice they reached the Pole on December 14th, 1911, one of the greatest feats of world exploration:

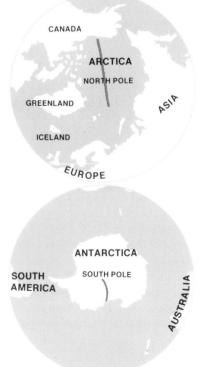

"Five roughened frostbitten fists it was gripped the post, lifted the fluttering flag on high and planted it together as the very first at the Geographic South Pole."

It was not only to the use of dogs that Amundsen owed his achievement (although he did realize the value of fresh meat, and used his dogs for both transport and fresh meat) but also that he was a man dedicated to exploration. His careful planning, together with experience, his endurance and single-mindedness helped him to achieve the speeds that enabled the Norwegians to reach the Pole with apparently so little trouble.

At the Pole they spent a day taking hourly observations and left a note in the tent which Scott was to find when he arrived 34 days later: Dear Captain Scott,

> As you probably are the first to reach this area after us, I will ask you kindly to forward this letter to King Haakon VII. If you can use any of the articles left in the tent please do not hesitate to do so. With kind regards I wish you a safe return.
>
> Yours truly
>
> Roald Amundsen

This must have been a bitter pill for Scott to swallow – to play postman for his victor – but it may be that Amundsen was safeguarding against his expedition not returning.

For Amundsen everything seemed to go well. On the whole they had fine weather, few blizzards, good surfaces – all making for easy sledging; they had plenty of food and the dogs even put on weight. Their journey there and back took only 99 days at an average speed of 19 miles (30 kilometres) a day – nearly 1,900 miles (3,000 kilometres) of the worst going in the world. The venture was described as bold, professional and successful. Although they had some frostbite they returned without sickness or injury. Much credit was due to their taking dogs and to their handling of them, although they were criticized by the English for their callousness. They took 52 and killed 24 to feed the others or themselves. The outcome was so different to that of Scott's expedition. He lost his life as did his companions in a tale beset with accident and illness.

Amundsen's airship the Norge over Oslo on its way to the North Pole.

With the funds Amundsen received from his Antarctic adventure he established a shipping business. Then he made another polar trip, this time through the North East Passage, before attempting another first – that of flying over the north Pole.

He flew within 170 miles (270 kilometres) in 1925 but was then beaten by Byrd in 1926, so that he was only "one of the first" when a few days later, he went over in an airship from Spitsbergen to Alaska with the Italian General Nobile.

In 1928 Nobile was lost on another flight. Although Amundsen had quarrelled with Nobile he set off to look for him. The seaplane he used in the search crashed in the polar seas and Amundsen was never heard of again.

Robert Falcon Scott

(1868–1912)

Scott in his "den" at McMurdo Sound – a small haven away from the bitter elements.

When Scott and his companions arrived at the South Pole on January 17th 1912 to discover that the Norwegian party had got there 34 days before them he wrote: "Great God! this is an awful place and terrible enough for us to have laboured to it without the reward of priority." Had his earlier expedition not dissuaded him from using dogs, the story of his exploration may well have been different.

Robert Falcon Scott was born near Plymouth where he was first taught by a governess. At 13 he passed as a cadet into Britannia Royal Naval College in Dartmouth. He stayed in the Navy until 1899 when he was offered the command of a National Antarctic expedition, an apparently surprising choice in view of his lack of scientific qualifications or experience of Polar regions.

He left on the *Discovery* in 1901 and entered McMurdo Sound to winter over in the shadow of the volcanoes Erebus and Terror. A hut about 36 feet (11 metres) square which had been sent from Australia in sections was erected as a shelter for returning sledge parties if the ship should break loose. It even had a covered verandah around it. This was to remain the base of their expedition for two years while they pursued their scientific work. Shackleton (see page 82), who was with the party, edited a *South Polar Times* to which everyone made contributions under a *nom de plume*. The first copy was presented to the Captain at dinner and a bottle of

cherry brandy was opened. They also spent their spare time having debates.

In 1902 Scott, Shackleton and Dr Wilson went south to the edge of the plateau as far as 82°16'33", more than 200 miles (320 kilometres) further south than anyone before them, but all three of them contracted scurvy, Wilson got snow blindness and Shackleton was badly ill, coughing and spitting blood. By the time they returned to base they had been away 93 days and had covered 960 miles (1,536 kilometres). They had found that the dogs had not proved successful. Shackleton, to his shame, was sent home because of his illness but he was reluctant to leave and never forgave Scott for his decision.

A year after the first journey Scott went over the plateau of Antarctica, and returned to England after three years away.

The Polar Expedition

In 1910 Scott made his quest for the Pole and set off on the *Terra Nova* with 65 men, 33 dogs, 19 Siberian ponies, three motor sledges and scientific equipment. They established their winter quarters at Cape Evans and discovered that Amundsen and his party were also making for the Pole. They left in November 1911, having spent time laying depots in the Autumn of 1910. The motor-sledges they took broke down and the ponies were shot for food.

The dogs were sent back with the support party while Scott, facing blizzards and very low temperatures, set out for the Pole with Captain Oates, Dr Wilson, Lieutenant Bowers and Petty Officer Edgar Evans. They made slow progress through temperatures of −23°F and on 16th January 1912 saw a small black speck ahead of them. It was one of several flags marking the South Pole and they knew they had been beaten in the race to the Pole. They arrived at 6.30 pm on the 17th and left early the next morning remarking that "there is very little that is different from the monotony of past days".

At first their progress back was reasonable until they reached the Beardmore Glacier where Scott collected rocks and fossils. On the barrier, temperatures of down to −47°F were recorded. A fall by Evans which possibly damaged his brain led to his weakness and ultimate death on 17th February. By this time the men were weak and they discovered when they reached the depots that the oil that they needed so badly had been lost, possibly through evaporation. Winds were strong and Captain Oates had such bad frostbite that his toes were black with gangrene. He knew he was holding back the remaining three members of the expedition. With his last thoughts being of his mother he took the legendary walk out into the whirling snow with the words "I am just going outside and may be some time". He was never seen again.

By the 29th March they were only 11 miles (18 kilometres) from One Ton Depot and the bad luck that seemed to dog them struck again. The relief party sent to find them had been held up by a blizzard from the 3rd to the 10th March – and then their shortage of dog food compelled them to return. Thus Scott was to write "We shall stick it out to the end, but we are getting weaker, of course, and the end cannot be far. It seems a pity, but I do not think I can write any more".

His last letter to his wife was unemotional and brave (almost, said one writer, as if he had done no more than miss his train) and his letter to the public was a moving tribute to his party: "Had we lived, I should have had a tale to tell of the hardihood, endurance and courage of my companions which would have stirred the heart of every Englishman. These rough notes and our dead bodies must tell the tale". It was eight months later that their bodies were found and outside the tent was a pile of 35 pounds of rocks that Scott had quarried at Beardmore. He had dragged them back through the agonies of his expedition, a testament to his duty and courage.

(Above) Scott's group at the South Pole with Amunden's tent.
(Left) The Terra Nova caught in pack ice.

Sir Ernest Henry Shackleton

(1874–1922)

Accounts of Ernest Shackleton vary from hero-worship to scorn. He was a man of strong personality who was not only either loved or hated by others, but either loved or hated others himself.

He was an Anglo-Irishman from a professional background but it was probably the Irish in him that was the cause of his failure to slip easily into the attitudes and prejudices of English upper-middle class society of his day.

After a conventional public school education he joined the Merchant Navy and in 1901 he applied successfully to join Scott's National Antarctic Expedition on the *Discovery*. This was the opportunity the ambitious young man was seeking, and his ambitions seemed about to be realized when Scott chose him to join in his attempt to reach the South Pole. The expedition failed and Shackleton's health failed him too and he had to be pulled back part of the way on a sledge about which he felt very ashamed. His ill health and a clash of personalities with Scott meant that he was sent back to England before the end of the expedition.

Domestic responsibilities took over for the next few years until he found someone to back an Antarctic expedition of his own. A furious row now blew up with Scott who claimed that he had prior right to explore the South Pole and

when Shackleton left, relations between the two explorers remained strained.

This time his expedition almost succeeded. He noted in his diary of 9 January 1909, at 88° South "We have shot our bolt". Dogged by dysentery and not helped by another clash of personalities within his team, he was forced to turn back 100 miles (160 kilometres) from the South Pole. In other respects, however, the expedition was a success. The magnetic South Pole was reached and Mount Erebus climbed. Shackleton went home to a hero's welcome and a knighthood.

Amundsen's and Scott's success three years later (see pages 78 and 80) forced him to set his sights higher; not just at the South Pole but at "the largest and most striking of Polar journeys – to go right across the continent".

This time things went worse than ever before. His ship, the *Endurance*, was caught in pack ice before reaching land and Shackleton was forced to drift northwards, away from Antarctica for nine months. When the ice thawed the battered *Endurance* was abandoned. The party had first to reach the open sea. Shackleton then saw it as his duty to sail for help. This he did in one of the open boats with five other men. Although the

Shackleton (on the right) outside his tent.

Falkland Islands were closer, he chose to sail with the westerlies to South Georgia, 800 miles (1,280 kilometres) away, through one of the most treacherous seas in the world. Remarkably they survived, to land on the uninhabited south coast of South Georgia. The exhausted men now faced a trek across the frozen mountains at the island's heart.

Leaving three men behind, Shackleton set off and finally reached the safety of a whaling station. After three attempts he managed to rescue every single one of his men.

Shackleton was not a well man, in spite of the active life he led. In 1922, on his next expedition to the Antarctic he died suddenly of a heart attack in South Georgia, and was buried there at his wife's request. It was an appropriate final resting place.

(*Above*) *Mount Erebus had already inspired James Clark Ross to paint the mountain in its Antarctic setting. Here, the mountain has been painted in a quieter mood by Wilson as it appeared when he and Shackleton accompanied Scott on his epic expedition.*

(*Left*) *The crew of Shackleton's ship Endurance attempt to cut a path for it through the pack-ice of the Weddell Sea. Although a passage which had been cut earlier is visible the ice has reformed.*

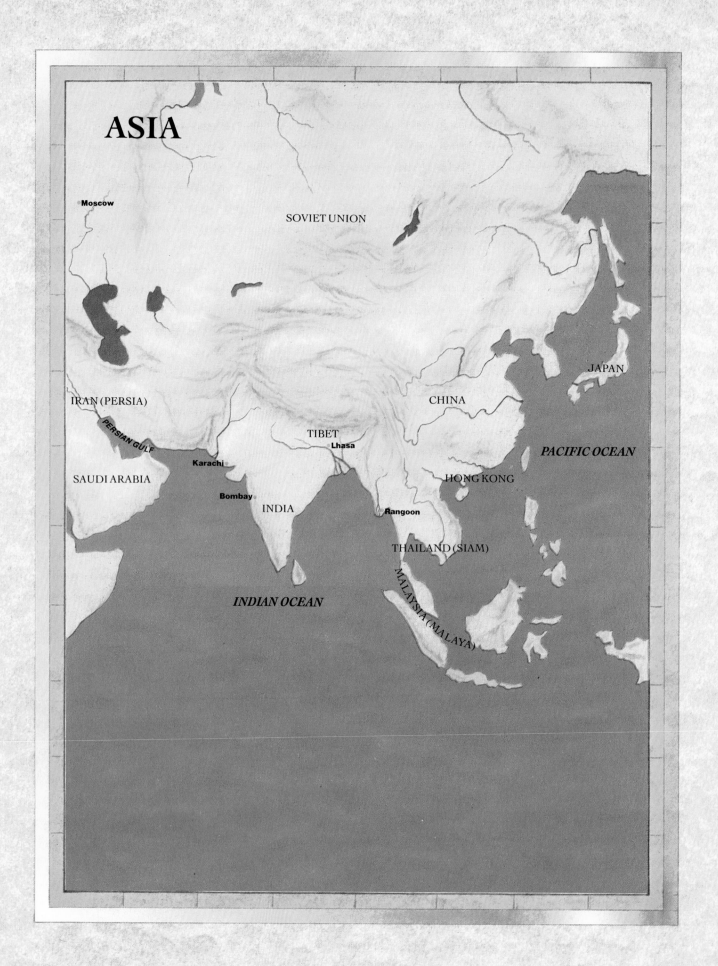

ASIA

Moscow

SOVIET UNION

JAPAN

IRAN (PERSIA)

CHINA

PERSIAN GULF

TIBET

Lhasa

PACIFIC OCEAN

Karachi

SAUDI ARABIA

HONG KONG

Bombay

INDIA

Rangoon

THAILAND (SIAM)

INDIAN OCEAN

MALAYSIA (MALAYA)

Johann Greuber & Albert d'Orville ASIA

(Greuber 1623–1680, d'Orville 1623–1662)

Fathers Johann Greuber and Albert d'Orville were most likely the first Europeans ever to reach Lhasa, in Tibet, travelling from Peking, and were almost certainly the first to see Mount Everest on their epic journey from China to India overland cutting directly across the formidable Himalayan Mountains.

They were both Jesuits, a religious order known for courage and intelligence which often made them the vanguard for the explorers who came later.

Johann Greuber, a first class mathematician and theologian, volunteered to work in China and on his trip out to the China Mission travelled overland via the Persian Gulf. The Mission was administered by an unorthodox priest who was very interested in science.

When the Chinese Emperor died the Vatican requested a meeting between themselves and members of the Chinese Mission. Greuber, an Austrian, with his youth, geographical knowledge and experience in travel was chosen to go. As the Dutch controlled the sea routes Greuber decided to travel overland and to explore the Tibetan Highlands.

With him went Albert d'Orville, a count, who had left his Belgian homeland and volunteered to go to China to follow his religious career.

They set off from Peking in April 1661 armed with Imperial passports and surveying equipment. They followed an ancient caravan route to Sining-Fu where the Great Wall of China was "so broad that six horsemen may run abreast on it". From there they struck out across the Tartar Desert, around the brackish lake Koko Nor, and across the dry plains of Mongolia where the "bleak hillsides are broken only by the occasional cluster of black felt tents, home of the predatory Mongols!"

After crossing a pass 15,000 feet (4,575 metres) high and a world of "dessicated rock and unremitting wind" they reached Lhasa – the Forbidden City, capital of Tibet. No European had been there for more than 300 years.

After spending a month there Greuber and d'Orville tackled the worst part of the journey. They crossed mountains through a pass nearly 17,000 feet (5,180 metres) high. They used flimsy Tibetan suspension bridges across yawn-

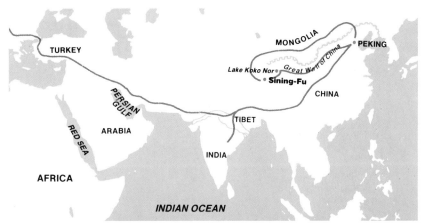

ing chasms and perilous toeholds suspended over gorges 1,500 feet (457 metres) deep, but eventually reached Agra in India almost a year after leaving Peking. At Mogar Mission the exhausted d'Orville died a few weeks later and was buried in the Martyr's Chapel.

Greuber went on to Rome by way of Persia and Turkey and though he planned to return to China his health prevented it and he spent some years as an army chaplain with the Imperial Austrian troops in Transylvania. He died in Hungary, aged 57.

Travelling through Central Asia was perilous at the time of Grueber and D'Orville. Not only was the terrain inhospitable but they also had to rely on flimsy craft to cross lakes and rivers. In the mountainous areas they would also encounter drift-ice which made crossings more dangerous, especially if it had to be done at night.

Hsuan-Tsang
(c.602–664)

In the 16 years that Hsuan-Tsang was engaged on the greatest travels the world had yet seen, time and again his fortunes swung from being feted with great pomp and honour to being set upon by brigands and thieves.

His journeys from China had been started when, after studying Buddhist works in the monasteries of China, he felt he needed to "travel to the countries of the West, in order to question the wise men on the points that were troubling his mind", as the writings he had studied did not agree with one another.

When he sought permission from the Emperor to leave it was refused, and after a dream in which he was able to climb a divine mountain with the help of a lotus stone and a whirlwind, he left secretly from Liang-Chou near the Great Wall to cross the Gobi Desert. Deserted by his companions and guide he followed the bones and droppings of camels. Because of his isolation in the desert his mind played tricks and he thought he saw marching troops with camels and decorated horses, lances and standards. After receiving help at a frontier post he lost his way and dropped his water skin. For four nights and five days he was without water until his horse scented some and saved them both.

He was welcomed by the King of Turfan who was reluctant for him to continue on his way so that Hsuan-Tsang had to threaten a hunger strike before, with an escort and presents for the Great Khan of the Western Turks, he was allowed to carry on his quest. He observed very carefully as he went, the customs, products and climates of the country he passed through and was able to convey a great deal of knowledge later to the Chinese Emperor. On one occasion Tripitaka (Three Bags Full) as he was called, met 2000 mounted Turkish bandits; on another Buddha's shadow in a cave chased away some robbers; and in his travels in India Hsuan-Tsang collected many relics and sacred texts to do with Buddha – "a tooth, even a fingernail . . . his stick and his begging bowl".

Captured for Sacrifice

He also visited Bodh-Gaya, which is where the Buddha had attained Enlightenment.

In the sacred Ganges valley he found doctors of the law and great libraries full of sacred books.

Near what is now Allahabad he fell prey to pirates who, following their custom of sacrificing a handsome young man to their goddess, had forced him to mount an altar they had built. At that moment a cyclone blew up, capsizing their boat, and they prostrated themselves before Hsuan-tsang, begging his forgiveness.

When he travelled up the Ganges River with the King of Assam, King Harsha, he was part of a procession of 20,000 elephants and 30,000 boats.

He waited many months for permission from China to return to his homeland, but when permission came he had great trouble in leaving India, so well known had he become. When he did finally leave he was given a wide variety of gifts from an elephant to silver and gold The elephant was to prove a great deal of trouble as it

The complex writing system which had been developed by the Chinese by the time of Hsuan-Tsang reflects the early civilization of China. Buddhism was then, and still is, the main religion in China as religious statuettes made throughout the centuries testify.

was difficult to carry enough food to feed it. Each day it ate some 40 bundles of hay and over 20 pounds of buns. Eventually near the Pamirs, as they were fleeing from some robbers, it hurled itself into a river. Probably Hsuan-Tsang's party heaved a sigh of relief. The elephant had carried him safely across the Indus while the monks accompanying him carried his precious manuscripts by boat. As the boat was in midstream stormy waters tipped it so that 50 manuscripts and some flower seeds were washed away. When the King of Kapisi met him he asked him immediately the question as to whether he had carried any flower seeds with him and when told the answer, he said "Whoever tries to cross the river with flower seeds suffers the same accident". They managed however to get copies of the manuscripts.

In all Hsuan-Tsang brought back 657 different volumes of manuscripts, six statues of Buddha and 150 particles of Buddha's flesh, in spite of the fact that he had written to the Emperor that because his elephant had been drowned he had not been able to bring back as much as he wanted!

As well as the knowledge and accounts of travel Hsuan-Tsang had brought back to China, he had also made a priceless contribution to Buddhism and he founded a school of Buddhism that is still acknowledged today. On his return to China he had found it hard, because of the calls upon him as a famous celebrity, to escape to translate all the texts he had brought.

In 664 he had a fall which troubled him until his death that year.

*(**Above**) The pageantry which Hsuan-Tsang saw when travelling with the King of Assam is evident from this picture which shows two potentates meeting on the Ganges. (**Right**) Horse-drawn vehicles were very much a status symbol in 7th century China.*

The Buddha depicted in the 17th Century.

Sir Francis Younghusband

(1863–1942)

In 1889 a young Englishman called Francis Younghusband was on a mission to the mountainous Karakoram in North-west India to investigate attacks by raiders from a remote mountain kingdom, when he came face to face with a Russian officer. It was a symbolic confrontation. These were the days when the Himalayan region was a buffer between the Russian and British Empires. The struggle to gain influence over the warlike tribes of this remote and hostile region was known as "The Great Game".

As part of the "Game" the British Government in India encouraged its most adventurous young men to explore the "Roof of the World" and beyond. Francis Younghusband was one of these men.

At the age of 24 he became the first European since Marco Polo to cross the Gobi Desert and returned through the Himalayas by a previously unknown route.

Younghusband was to meet another Russian in 1891 who ordered him off what he claimed was "Russian Territory". This encounter led to a diplomatic row and an eventual agreement between Britain and Russia over territorial claims.

Younghusband's most important task was to lead a military mission to Tibet, which had been causing trouble for the British along its Himalayan borders. His job was to "show the flag" and to secure a treaty.

His success at this and in his travels generally was probably due to the fact that he had made a close study of Hinduism and Buddhism. He was also brave, and once rode unarmed into a Tibetan armed camp to talk to the commander.

In his old age he became an active supporter of British expeditions to climb Mount Everest.

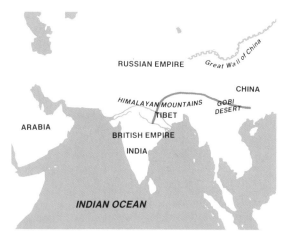

Younghusband (left) and his two companions on his journey across the Gobi Desert.

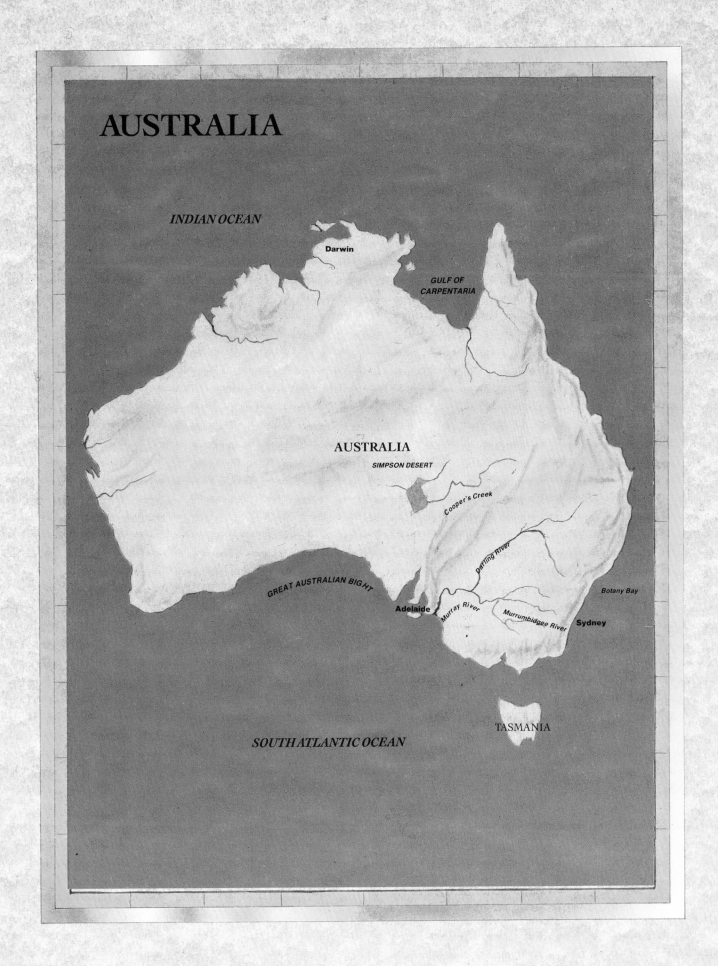

AUSTRALIA

INDIAN OCEAN

Darwin

GULF OF
CARPENTARIA

AUSTRALIA

SIMPSON DESERT

Cooper's Creek

Darling River

GREAT AUSTRALIAN BIGHT

Adelaide

Murray River

Murrumbidgee River

Botany Bay

Sydney

TASMANIA

SOUTH ATLANTIC OCEAN

Charles Sturt
(1795–1869)

Charles Sturt was in the early days following his exploits described by some people as a mere traveller and it was some time before the accolades he justly deserved such as "father of Australian exploration" and "one of the most distinguished explorers and geographers of our day" were accorded to him.

He was a pleasant, modest but sickly man whose expeditions did not bring him the immediate fame of other explorers and shortly before his death he was to write to Sir George Grey, "I am however so used to disappointment . . . that I

A contemporary painting of Sturt surveying a desert landscape, 1829.

hardly expect success in any way".

After travelling to Canada and to Ireland in his early military life he was promoted to Captain in 1825 and set out for Sydney in Australia to guard the convicts who had been sent to the colony. Despite his onerous task he was to enjoy "a climate so soft that man scarcely requires a dwelling, and so enchanting that few have left it without regret".

In 1828 he led an expedition which reached the River Darling and was inspired to undertake a second expedition in 1829 when he reached the River Murrumbidgee and sailed down it to the Murray and thence to the sea passing the River Darling on the way. By the time he and his party had returned they had travelled 1500 miles (2400 kilometres) and had discovered the fertile lands of south Australia. They had also shown the way for channels of water communication and solved the southeast water system of Australia.

Blindness saw Sturt return to England on sick leave. Fortunately his sight was restored and he returned to Australia.

Disappointed at not being given the colonial secretaryship he desired, he set out from Adelaide in August 1844 to try to reach the centre of Australia. He had with him 15 men, six dogs, 11 horses, 30 bullocks, 200 sheep and a boat.

The expedition failed to reach the centre by only 150 miles (240 kilometres), but they mapped 100,000 square miles (256,000 square kilometres) of some of the "most desolate territory on earth" and all except one person came back alive. Sturt had reached the edge of the Simpson Desert and sensibly realized he could go no further. When he and his party returned, "gaunt indeed were the wanderers, their faces hidden in unkempt hair, their skin burnt almost to the swarthy hue of the natives. The horses were like living skeletons and many of the cattle in sorry plight". Sturt, suffering from scurvy had had to be carried part of the way in a dray.

Blindness forced Sturt to early retirement and he settled in Cheltenham. He heard in May 1869 that he had been awarded a Knighthood but died before the honour was made public. His honour was "for the prudence with which further advance was abandoned" – a negative but important feat.

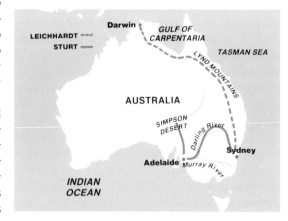

Friedrich Wilhelm Ludwig Leichhardt

(1813–1849)

Friedrich Leichhardt was not the sort of person one would expect to be an explorer. An eccentric German scholar of slight physique, he had such poor eyesight that he never carried a gun because he couldn't see well enough to hit anything.

He arrived in Australia from Europe in 1842 at the age of 28 and became known as a botanist and natural historian. When an overland expedition which he had applied to join failed to materialize he decided to lead his own expedition with the financial encouragement of businessmen and farmers who were on the look-out for productive lands.

He set out in September 1844 with what has been described as "the most dubious band of explorers in Australian annals" for what he thought would be a five-month journey but which in the event took almost 15 months: "What will people say when I appear suddenly resurrected from the grave with a heap of mountain ranges, rivers and creeks in my pocket?".

Although they endured hardships such as lack of food – they had sometimes to eat leaves and chew leather – the country was not inhospitable in the way Sturt's trip had been. Leichhardt wrote of "fine country covered with grass, and herbs well-watered. Open forests and plains well-stocked with game, honey sweet as that of Hymettus, and the air fragrant with thyme and marjoram". In the Lynd mountains Leichhardt's party came upon a recently-deserted camp and found four kangaroo nets. As they needed the twine they took two of them and left as payment 4 fishhooks, a silk handkerchief and a sword with a hilt of polished brass.

Some of the party became eager to turn back but they soon came upon a great waterhole where they rested and celebrated an early Christmas by killing a bullock. For the real Christmas meal they had stewed cockatoo and suet pudding.

Later one of their party was killed in a skirmish with hostile natives. Another received six spears in him – three in the scalp, one in the cheek, one through the left arm and one in the groin as well as being clubbed in the shoulder. Miraculously he survived.

At last in December 1845 they rode into Port Essington near Darwin looking "like scarecrows" and eventually sailed back to Sydney by schooner to be greeted as though raised from the dead. Leichhardt had paved the way for opening up the northeast.

The money he received for this venture he put towards another to cross Australia from east to west and in December 1846 he set off with seven men, 70 animals and their equipment. Within 500 miles (800 kilometres) most of their animals were gone, the men were despairing, fever was rife and the waterholes had dried up. He

returned amid criticisms of being clumsy and overbearing, selfish and greedy and some even thought him mad.

Despite this failure he set off again, undaunted, only a few weeks after he had returned. He had decided to follow the Barcoo River as far as the Gulf of Carpentaria, then head for the west coast. What he did not realize was that the Barcoo eventually swung west where it disappeared into the desert and the many holes of Cooper's Creek. He was never heard of again and though many theories and stories were put forward, his end remains a mystery to this day.

*(**Top**) The Australian Aborigine was far better equipped for survival in the outback than were the European pioneers. (**Above**) A contemporary ink sketch of Leichhardt.*

John McDouall Stuart

(1815–1866)

If John McDouall Stuart had not been a puny sickly child he would no doubt have joined the army as his father and forbears had done before him. As it was, although dogged by ill health throughout his life he was to become the first person to lead an expedition across Australia, through its centre from north to south, and return.

When Stuart arrived in Australia he worked at a survey camp and no doubt liked the bush life and was certainly drawn to the barren interior. He found it enthralling and was to show great skill in bushmanship in the many expeditions he undertook.

In 1844 he joined Charles Sturt's expedition (see page 90) to try to reach the centre of Australia and learned of the sorts of hardships that had to be endured. He had to deal with the "heat in which the skin was burnt off the feet of the dogs, boxes fell to pieces, and ink dried on the pen before a word could be written". Despite his reputation as a drinker, Sturt found him invaluable on the trip.

In 1858 Stuart set out with one white man and one Aboriginal on horses and discovered Cooper's Creek where there seemed to be permanent water. This was to be a useful base when he later crossed Australia. On this first expedition he travelled 800 miles (1,280 kilometres) through unexplored territory. Despite his illnesses he showed great courage and skill in the bush, and was received with acclaim on his return – another much better equipped expedition had not made the progress he had. He then went on to examine the area he had travelled and his thoughts turned to the discovery of gold. At that time, too, people were starting to talk about the possibility of a telegraph line across the country.

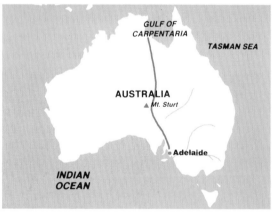

His First Major Achievement

In 1860, only 24 years after the first official settlers had come to Australia, Stuart and his two companions reached the spot which they determined as the centre of Australia and planted a flag to mark their achievement. Stuart generously named the spot Mount Sturt after his predecessor.

Despite clashes with the Aborigines and continuous scurvy Stuart was undaunted. Even though a further expedition had seen his party so hungry that they were pleased to get a lizard or kite to eat to supplement their diet of wild plants, fruits and berries, he set off again in 1862 with 10 men and over 70 horses.

Some six months after leaving Adelaide he reached the Gulf of Carpentaria. The six months spent on the return trip were a nightmare of scurvy and blindness for Stuart, followed by a stroke. An improvised stretcher carried between two horses took him part of the way and the

party all had to contend with low provisions, little water and their own and their horses' weakness.

Nevertheless on 21st January 1863 a "hairy undersized skeleton of a man, his bush clothing in tatters, rode in triumph at the head of the equally ragged little group" into Melbourne to confirm that they had crossed through the centre of the continent from sea to sea and back.

Instead of the acknowledgement he deserved, Stuart received little recompense or honour for his achievement and returned to England half-blind and half-crippled, even though his efforts were largely responsible for the telegraph route, the railway to the interior and the highway.

(Centre) Travelling through unexplored territory where the white man had never before been seen, Stuart and his companions encountered hostile aborigines.
(Below) Six months after leaving Adelaide, Stuart planted his flag on the ocean shore on the far side of the continent.

(1820–1861)

A Race! A race! So great a one
The world ne'er saw before;
A race! A race across this land
From south to northern land

These few lines from the *Melbourne Herald* show the circumstances in which the attempt to cross Australia led to the tragedy that awaited Burke and his party.

The Australian county of Victoria had backed Burke's expedition, having chosen Burke no doubt for his charm, bravery and sense of adventure, while South Australia had backed John McDouall Stuart in a similar venture (see page

Burke, Wills and King return to Cooper's Creek.

92). So on 20th August, 1860 Burke set out with Wills, his second-in-command, 14 other men, 27 camels, and 23 horses. "It was exactly a quarter to four when the expedition got into marching order." By October they had quarrelled and split up. One group went on to Cooper's Creek and set up a depot close by a waterhole, and a further split led to Burke, Wills and two other companions, King and Gray, setting off on their own for the Gulf of Carpentaria nearly 1000 miles (1,600 kilometres) northwards.

They crossed Sturt's stony desert which was at that time "green and luxuriant" and 57 days after leaving Cooper's Creek they reached the Gulf. They were not, in fact, able to see the sea because of the floods and thunderstorms, but it was only a few miles away.

By this time rations were low, they were weak and had scurvy. Food dominated their

thoughts on their return journey and when Gray was discovered eating some gruel, saying that he had dysentery, he was beaten. The party did not realize that he was dying.

He travelled to within 70 miles (112 kilometres) of the Cooper's Creek depot before he died. When the rest of the party reached Cooper's Creek on the 21st April, it was to discover that the depot party had left that morning despite their instructions to the contrary. Imagine the despair of Burke's party at reading the message left buried in a bottle by Willam Brahe. Wills wrote, "Our disappointment may be easily imagined – returning in an exhausted state", since "our two camels are done up, and we shall not be able to travel further than 4 or 5 miles (7 or 8 kilometres) a day". Burke felt they ought not to try to catch up with the depot party and they tried, after eating the provisions left for them, to make their way down Cooper's Creek. They had to shoot their camels which got bogged down in the swamps and went back toward the Creek where Aborigines tried to restore them with fish and nardoo seed and pitchery – a kind of drug. Wills urged the other two on and died about 1st July, Burke a few days later. King, the only survivor was found three months later half-mad with starvation and loneliness.

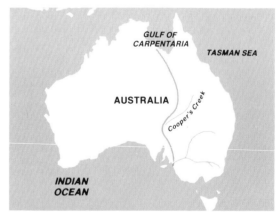

THE
OCEANS

Joshua Slocum

(1844–1909)

Slocum was born on 20th February, 1844, in Nova Scotia. There had been sailors on both sides of his family, although his father was, in fact, a farmer. The sea was obviously in Joshua's blood from the start, and, although he turned his hand to a number of jobs, it was the sea that ultimately brought him both fulfilment and renown. "Joshua, as a small boy, while working 'on the old clay farm which some calamity had made his father's', could hear in the distance before him the roaring of the tides. At his back was the Annapolis River valley. He could look down and see the tall spruce trees good for building ships. In the time between farm chores and meagre country schooling, he built a raft out of spruce fence rails, put a sail on it, and sallied forth across the mill pond. Whenever he could he joined the neighbours fishing for cod and mackerel in the bay. From the start he was obsessed with ships."

At the age of ten Joshua found himself helping his father to make fishermen's leather boots. He hated doing this, and took every opportunity to go down to the cellar, where he was working secretly on the model of a sailing ship. Eventually his father found out what had been going on, and such was his fury that he smashed the model to pieces. After this Joshua broke with his father. The incident had probably been the last straw in an unsatisfactory relationship.

Joshua, when he was 14, became a cook on a fishing schooner. Unfortunately, his culinary skills (or rather lack of them) were not entirely to the satisfaction of the crew, so he gave this up and became a deep-sea sailor, plying between the major ports of the world. Whenever he had

a spare moment he studied, practised with the sextant, and learned navigation.

Slocum's first proper voyage was to Hong Kong via Dublin and Liverpool. Many others followed. He eventually became an American citizen, and made San Francisco his base. At this point he started shipbuilding, although he was still actually a sailor. In 1869, when he was only 25, Slocum was given his first command, becoming captain of a coasting schooner plying between San Francisco and Seattle. Next came the bark *Washington*, on which he sailed to Sydney and then Alaska. He even honeymooned on board *Washington*, sailing across the Pacific on this same route in search of salmon! Unfortunately the ship dragged her anchors in a gale, and was stranded on the shoals, some two hundred miles (320 kilometres) from Kodiak. A whaleboat had to be used to transfer everything to another ship.

Solo Voyage Planned

The *Constitution* was Slocum's next command. This ship was a small packet running between San Francisco and Honolulu. His first child – a boy – was born on board the *Constitution* in San Francisco harbour. For a time after this Slocum devoted his energies to shipbuilding, setting up a primitive boatyard at Olongape, a jungle village 60 miles (96 kilometres) from Manila. He was, however, to make many further voyages and command other vessels before embarking upon his circumnavigation of the world. On one trip to Hong Kong on board the schooner *Pato* his family accompanied him, treating the ship as their home.

Captain Joshua Slocum said of his circumnavigation of the world "The voyage was the natural outcome not only of my love of adventure, but of my lifelong experience." **(Right)** *His sloop, Spray, in which he completed the voyage.*

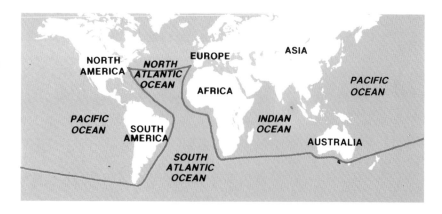

Although the idea of sailing alone round the world had been in Slocum's mind for many years ("Nobody knows just when or how he got the idea, but from the beginning, perhaps unawares, he had been preparing for it"), it was really only when a whaling friend by the name of Captain Pierce gave Slocum an ancient oyster sloop (possibly one hundred years old) called *The Spray* that he began to work seriously towards this end. "By dint of hard work, steady application, and some skill at shipbuilding" he managed to rebuild the craft entirely. This took thirteen months. "She was 36 feet 9 inches (11.2 metres) overall, 14 feet 2 inches (4.3 metres) wide, and 4 feet 2 inches (1.27 metres) deep in the hold. Her gross tonnage was just under 13 tons."

At about this time there was Civil War in Brazil, and Slocum wrote his book *Voyage of the Destroyer from New York to Brazil.*

Under Way

The start of any great voyage is always an exciting time. So much planning is involved. Next comes the actual loading-up of the ship or boat. Slocum was fortunate to be given supplies by the grocers and other tradesmen of Boston. In addition he took revolvers and rifles. Clearly Slocum was not unduly concerned about matters of health since he took "only the simplest of medicines and some disinfectants". He did, however, take with him charts "for all over the world", a sextant, a compass, a chronometer and a patent "log" for measuring speed and distance.

Slocum set sail at the age of 51, from East Boston, on 24th April, 1895. The voyage is described in the book *Sailing Alone Around the World* which Slocum afterwards wrote. He had many adventures on the trip, including being chased by Moorish pirates off the coast of Morocco. Just over three years after setting off, Slocum anchored at Newport, on 27th June, 1898, after crossing the Atlantic to Gibraltar, and thence going west, through the Magellan Straits, across the Pacific to Australia, round the Cape of Good Hope, and so with a third crossing of the Atlantic, completing his circumnavigation of the world.

On 14th November, 1909, Slocum set off on board *The Spray* from Vineyard Haven, bound probably for Menemsha, but failed to make his port of call. No trace of Slocum or his boat was found.

Thor Heyerdahl
(b.1914)

Kon-Tiki Sets Sail

Heyerdahl and his companions (five men and a parrot) flew to South America to find suitable balsa trees and to build the now-famous raft. The raft was named on 27th April 1947 – *Kon-Tiki* and on the 28th it was towed out to sea for the start of the voyage.

The members of the expedition had many adventures on the way. They saw many of the natural life of the sea at first hand – dolphins, the very rare snake mackerel, huge sea-turtles, birds and the dramatic appearance of a giant whale shark. The whale shark is the largest shark and largest fish known to man – even a baby whale shark has been found to have 3,000 teeth! Knowing the danger they were in one of the crew eventually thrust a harpoon into the head of the whale shark which disappeared into the ocean never to be seen again.

Numerous problems beset them on the voyage including a fire caused by the Primus stove they carried with them, and infestation of ants aboard the raft and storms and gales. The raft was finally wrecked on a coral reef at Raroia which Heyerdahl and his companions found to be a South Sea island-paradise. Soon, Polynesians from other islands came and transported them to their own, inhabited islands and they were given a tremendous reception. What remained of the *Kon-Tiki* was hauled ashore. This is now restored and can be seen among other exhibits of Heyerdahl's travels at the Kon-Tiki Museum in Oslo.

Other expeditions which Heyerdahl took part in were just as important as the Kon-Tiki one although perhaps not quite as famous. In 1952 he organized and led an expedition to the Galapagos Islands and an archaeological expedition to Easter Island. In 1970 Heyerdahl crossed from Morocco to the West Indies in a papyrus boat, *Ra II*.

*(**Right**) At Gizeh in Egypt, Ra II was built and rolled across the desert, a technique of the Pharoahs.*

Thor Heyerdahl was born in Norway and educated at the University of Oslo and has been an author and anthropologist since 1938. In the late 1930s he carried out research in the Marquesas Islands of the Pacific and then among the Coast Indians of British Columbia. He saw active service during World War II in the free Norwegian Army-Air Force parachute unit.

It was shortly after the war that Heyerdahl organized and led the expedition which brought him world-wide fame – the Kon-Tiki Expedition. Heyerdahl's intention was to test out a theory that Inca people had drifted across the sea from Peru to Polynesia on balsa-wood craft. Heyerdahl wanted to see if a replica craft had the performance and quality needed for such a journey and whether the wind and currents really would propel it across the sea with the crew still on board. By taking part in the actual trip, he would find out whether the crew could get fresh fish and rainwater while crossing the ocean.

Thor Heyerdahl, seen above with some of his international crew, later added a mast and sail.

*(**Top**) The Ra under full sail.*

═══════════ *Sir Francis Chichester*
(*1901–1972*)

Francis Chichester on Gipsy Moth IV in which he sailed alone around the world.

Francis Chichester was born on 17th September, 1901. After being educated at Marlborough College he emigrated to New Zealand in 1919 in search of adventure, with ten pounds in sovereigns and a determination not to return until he had made £20,000. After trying his hand at many jobs, among them farm-work, sheep-shearing, timber-sawing and coal and gold-mining, he founded a business with a New Zealand partner, and by the age of twenty-six had an income of £10,000 a year. He then turned his fertile mind to aviation, and in 1928 founded the Godwin-Chichester Aviation Co Ltd. After learning to fly, he returned to England, studied aerial navigation, bought a Gipsy Moth light aeroplane, and in December, 1929 and January 1930 he became the second man to fly solo from Britain to Australia.

In 1930 Chichester joined the New Zealand (Territorial) Air Force. His flying achievements include the first East to West solo flight from New Zealand to Australia across the Tasman Sea, for which he was awarded the Johnston Memorial Trophy for 1931 for Navigation; the first long-distance solo seaplane flight, from New Zealand to Japan, in 1931; and the Cruising Flight in Puss Moth with one passenger, from Sydney to London via Peking, in 1936. During World War II, from 1941 to 1945 he served in the RAF, and was Senior Navigation Officer at the Empire Central Flying School, from 1943 to 1945. His writing of books on aircraft identification prior to his appointment had clearly impressed the RAF authorities.

From Flying to Sailing

Chichester, who had already done some sailing, took it up again seven years after the war. However in 1957 he had a serious illness. Chichester drew upon spiritual resources in his successful fight against his illness.

A number of sailing successes were achieved by Francis Chichester before he embarked upon his most demanding and challenging enterprise. He won the first Singlehanded Transatlantic Yacht Race, from Plymouth to New York, in 1960. For this he was awarded the Yachtsman of the Year Trophy, 1960. He achieved a record solo East-West crossing, from Plymouth to New York in 1962. He also came second in the second Solo Transatlantic Yacht Race in 1964. However it is for the First Solo Circumnavigation of the World via the Capes of Good Hope, Leeuwin and Horn, 1966–67, that Chichester will go down in history. In addition, this was the fastest true circumnavigation, port to port, by any small boat: 29,600 miles (47,360 kilometres) in 226 days' sailing-time, Plymouth-Sydney-Plymouth. Chichester set sail on 27th August, 1966, and reached home again on 28th May, 1967.

On the voyage there were good days and bad ones. At the start, Chichester suffered from sea-sickness and a leg injury. He encountered gales, storms, contrary winds and baffling calms. On November 15th, in the Southern Indian Ocean, disaster struck. After three days of heavy gales, an essential part of the self-steering gear broke. Chichester, however, contrived and rigged up a self-steering arrangement of his own design.

Chichester was knighted by the Queen, using Drake's sword, at Greenwich on 7th July, 1967. Many other awards came his way, and further successes followed. He died on 26th August, 1972.

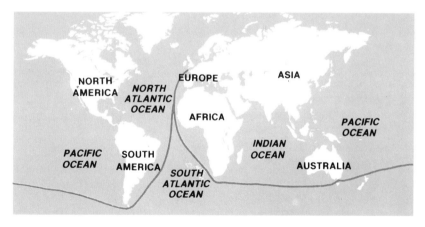

======== *Sir Alec Rose* ========

(b.1908)

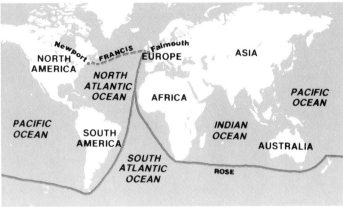

The distant figure of Alec Rose aboard the tiny Lively Lady in which he made his historic voyage.

The 1960's were golden years for daring enterprises in two fields in particular – those of space-exploration and navigation. As far as the latter is concerned, probably the best-remembered name is that of Sir Francis Chichester (see page 100), but another to hit the headlines within a short space of time was that of Alec (later Sir Alec) Rose.

Like many other men of adventure – explorers, mountaineers and navigators – Alec Rose had led a very varied life before embarking upon the enterprise which brought him fame and publicity. He was educated at a school in Canterbury, farmed in Canada for two years, and then became a haulage contractor. After serving in the RNVR during World War II he took up market-gardening, and was, for a time, a fruit-merchant.

It had been Alex Rose's youthful ambition to go to sea, and he now took up sailing, converting a ship's lifeboat into a yacht in which he lived and cruised to the Low Countries. His first deep-water success came in 1964 when he was placed fourth in the Singlehanded Transatlantic Race.

In 1968 Alec Rose circumnavigated the world in his boat *Lively Lady*. He had originally set off on 6th August 1966, but scarcely had he set sail than he was beset by a chapter of disasters. There was trouble with the engine, the steering-blade of the self-steering gear snapped off short, and to crown everything, *Lively Lady* was struck by a large ship. She was so badly damaged that it was necessary to have her repaired at Plymouth. There were further problems, and eventually Alec Rose came to the conclusion that the voyage would simply have to be postponed. He set sail a second time from Portsmouth on 16th July 1967.

Storm Damage

Alec Rose had to surmount such difficulties as straining himself, and having to weather many gales (*Lively Lady* was almost dismasted in one of these). She was again damaged in the storms of the Southern Ocean, so repairs had to be carried out in New Zealand before rounding Cape Horn could be contemplated. It was in the Southern Ocean, too, that on one occasion a huge whale surfaced close to *Lively Lady*, while in the South Atlantic he picked up flying-fish off the deck and fried them in butter for breakfast.

By the time he reached home again, on 4th July 1968, Alec Rose had been at sea for 318 days. He was given a great reception, and was knighted by the Queen at Buckingham Palace. Other honours also came Alec Rose's way, including the Freedom of Portsmouth, the Blue Water Medal of the Cruising Club of America and the Seamanship Medal of the Royal Cruising Club. In 1968 he published an autobiographical book entitled *My Lively Lady*.

Clare Francis, an attractive, feminine and intelligent woman has faced challenges which would daunt the hardiest and most daring of men. By sheer grit and determination in the most adverse of conditions, she has proved that a woman can be just as capable as a man of competing against, and overcoming, the hazards posed by the physical world and the elements.

Her first experience of the sea was at a very early age when she was taken by her father on a seaside holiday. She went sailing with him and was terrified of the way in which the boat tipped over to one side as it shot through the water, the waves banging the hull. Shivering from the cold of the spray she cried until she reached land again. Some years later, all the fear of the sea gone, she became very interested in sailing and learned all the basic techniques. At the age of twelve she was given a small wooden dinghy in which she was allowed to sail some distance on her own. However, she once did sail further than she was allowed to – ". . . to the edge of a shipping channel a mile out from the shore. A strong tide was sweeping me towards the open sea and the waves were dangerously large for my undecked boat. An icy fear suddenly gripped me and, with my heart racing, I turned back for the shore, very frightened yet childishly exhilarated at my own daring."

The daring of Clare Francis made her into the excellent sailor she is today. Having been educated at the Royal Ballet School in London and later taken a university degree one would be forgiven for not considering Clare Francis to eventually be among the world's top sailors. In 1973 she crossed the Atlantic single-handed from Falmouth to Newport NJ in just 37 days. In 1974 she took part in the Round Britain Race and was placed third. Clare's aim in 1976 was to sail the Atlantic single-handed in the Trans-Atlantic race. She was sponsored by a British firm of jammakers after which she named her boat *Robertson's Golly*. On a trial cruise before the race the *Golly* met high waves and Clare and her companion heard a horrifying crack when the tiller split in two.

The Race started on 5th June 1976 and from a number of possible routes that she could take, Clare opted for the Northern Route. Even so, she had forgotten to take any gloves and her fingers suffered badly from cracks and swelling. She had to contend with many gales and storms and during one particularly severe storm she could only move around the deck on her hands and knees. Finding dry clothing became impossible. On another occasion she narrowly missed hitting icebergs which were perilously near but which she could not see because of the thick fog. She reached Newport NJ on 4th July 1976.

In 1977–78 she was fifth in the Whitbread Round the World Race in the *Accutrac* and was named first woman skipper. All her achievements were recognized in 1978 when she was awarded the MBE.

(***Above***) *Clare Francis battled with very severe storms on her epic race across the Atlantic.*

Although John Ridgway is perhaps best known for his rowing exploits his adventure centre in Ardmore attracts young people to sailing as well as to other sports.

cost in the region of £2,000. By good fortune, however, Ridgway was able to purchase one called the *Yorkshire Dory* for a mere £185! The next vitally important step was to find a suitable partner in the enterprise. Again fortune favoured Ridgway, in the person of Chay Blyth, a former member of the Parachute Regiment in which Ridgway had, himself, served as an officer. The two had known each other – indeed they had once won a canoe race from Reading to London – a distance of 70 miles!

Fitness and Training

The fitness and survival tests which Ridgway had previously undergone in various parts of the world now stood him in good stead as he and Blyth embarked upon a course of fitness and training for their marathon undertaking. Subsequently their boat, now re-named *English Rose III*, underwent her sea-trials off Portsmouth.

On 4th June, 1966, Ridgway and Blyth set off to row from Orleans, near Cape Cod, Massachusetts, to Britain. They achieved this in just over 91 days. In the course of this remarkable enterprise they encountered gales, a hurricane, whales, sharks and a possible sea-serpent. The

One only has to glance through the list of titles of the autobiographical books written by John Ridgway to realize that here is a man who has led a highly adventurous life in many parts of the world, and who has also achieved a notable success at home in establishing his "outward bound" centre in the wilds of Scotland. There is little doubt, however, but that Ridgway will go down in history for his amazing feat of rowing across the Atlantic from America to Ireland with his companion and former fellow-soldier, Chay Blyth.

The seeds of this amazing enterprise had been sown when John Ridgway learned that two men proposed to row across the Atlantic. Inspired by the ambition to compete against this pair, Ridgway set about trying to acquire a suitable boat. To have had one built would have

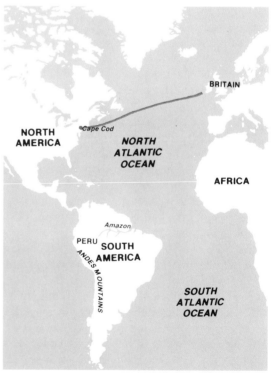

pair also established a remarkable relationship, the telepathy between them enabling each to sense what the other was thinking or feeling at any particular moment.

In the course of 91 days and nights in their 20 foot (6 metres) open boat, John Ridgway and his companion experienced fear and a variety of associated sensations as they were confronted by, for example, a whale which dived beneath their boat, a huge shark which appeared just as Ridgway was about to take a "dip" (it was at least as long as the boat itself), and "Hurricane Alma", which left them cold, wet and exhausted (they had had to bail frantically). In the aftermath of this, never had curry, rice and hot cocoa tasted better!

Another problem encountered was when Ridgway had a boil on his neck. This, however, turned into a humorous situation when Blyth pretended to "open" the boil, instead of which he simply applied a dressing!

Towards the end of the voyage the two men were beset by hunger, having had to reduce their rations by half. Fortunately the captain of a ship came to their aid. On 3rd September they reached Kilronan, Ireland, safely, at the end of

their remarkable voyage. Their rivals were not so fortunate, having been lost at sea.

In 1968 John Ridgway spent fifty days alone in a 30 foot (9 metres) yacht, the first of nine men to set out in a race to be the first person to sail round the world single-handed. This attempt failed as the result of a collision.

Return to Ardmore

Ridgway felt at this point that he should spend six months of the year in his remote croft home at Ardmore on the north-west coast of Scotland. He set about building a School of Adventure.

Some time later John Ridgway made another of his many exciting adventures. With two other men and a girl he had gone on an expedition in the high Andes, through the jungle, and then canoeing down the Amazon to the Atlantic, a distance of 4,000 miles (6,400 kilometres). In the course of this endeavour the party experienced vast changes of temperature ranging from the near-Arctic conditions of the Andes above 15,000 feet (4,570 metres), and the conditions found in the equatorial jungle. They had to negotiate rapids, and at one point their balsa-raft was wrecked, forcing them to transfer to a dug-out canoe. Many photographs, especially of the wild life, were taken during this expedition.

Since then John Ridgway has returned to the mountains of Peru, finding on this occasion a little girl whom he and his wife have now adopted.

John Ridgway, in foreground, steps ashore.

Jacques Cousteau
(b.1910)

Jacques Cousteau was born in 1910, not far from the port of Bordeaux. When he was ten he went with his family to New York for a year. He later trained at the Naval Academy, Brest. Subsequently he became Chief Officer of the French Naval Base at Shanghai. In France he suffered a serious accident when driving a sports car. One of his arms was seriously damaged, but through sheer perseverance Cousteau eventually regained the use of his arm and fingers. This experience led to an interest in the well-being of handicapped people, and he even employed one or two such people on his ship.

In 1938 Cousteau designed the oxygen rebreathing lung. This enables a diver's exhalations to be passed back into a bag and be repurified there, in soda lime, to be breathed again by the diver. Cousteau's first underwater film *Sixty Feet Down* was, however, made without the use of breathing apparatus.

Cousteau's interest in what lies beneath the ocean was initially aroused in the summer of 1939, when he was exploring the African seas off Tunisia. He was amazed by what he saw, but almost lost his life when he became trapped beneath an underwater platform with only half a minute to live. He was fortunate to find an escape-hole just in time.

Many wrecks were explored by Cousteau, in particular one at Grand Congloué island, which lies between Toulon and Marseilles. Bowls and other valuable finds from the 3rd Century BC

were discovered. It is, however, for his films of, and research on, underwater wild-life that Jacques Cousteau is renowned. On one occasion, when in the Indian Ocean, 600 miles (960 kilometres) east of Africa, he and his crew sighted whales. These had supposedly been exterminated in that particular area. Cousteau's ship *Calypso* actually hit one of the whales – a baby. It had been badly injured by the propeller blades, and was deserted and left to die by the other whales. One of the crewmen used a "harpoon of mercy" on the suffering creature, but at that point sharks appeared on the scene. The baby whale was then shot. Following this, Cousteau and a companion had themselves hoisted over the stern of the ship in a yellow anti-shark cage. They had with them aqua-lungs and a movie camera. A crane swung the cage away from the ship, and the two divers sank into the sea, attached to the ship only by a slender cable. Cousteau, in order to better film the sharks as

EUROPE
Marseilles• •Toulon
MEDITERRANEAN
TUNISIA

ASIA

AFRICA

INDIA Shanghai •

INDIAN
OCEAN

SOUTH
ATLANTIC
OCEAN

(*Above*) *Cousteau's ship
Calypso lies at anchor.*
(*Right*) *Habitat which
Cousteau built on the sea
bed near Port Sudan.
Researchers could live
underwater for days and
observe marine life and
the growth of the corals.*

they tore the dead whale to pieces, actually
opened the door of the cage!

This was just one of many hundreds of underwater adventures and discoveries many of
which, through the medium of television, have
been brought to a vast world-wide audience.
Annual oceanographic expeditions were made
by Cousteau and his companions on board the
Calypso and film records were kept from 1951
onwards.

Hans & Lotte Hass

(Dates not known)

Once underwater, the diver enters a totally different world. Silent wrecks, such as the Umbria, partly seen here, are an attraction to explorers like Hans Hass.

The name of Hans and Lotte Hass became familiar to television viewers in the 1950s, when films of the underwater diving activities, explorations and adventures of this famous couple were regular features.

Hans Hass was brought up in Vienna, but spent many interesting holidays on the Mediterranean Coast, particularly the French Riviera. When Hans was only four, his Uncle Fritz tried to teach him to swim. Hans almost drowned on this occasion. Four years later, however, he was taught to float, almost accidentally, by his mother. At about this time Hans discovered another fascinating and absorbing interest – that of hunting and collecting shells and coloured stones.

One day, when his mother was unable to supervise him since she was recovering from a bout of seasickness, Hans went off on his own. He met a man, who asked him to find snails, which he proceeded to use as bait for fish. The man used a fork to catch the fish. Then he built a stove out of stones, and the pair enjoyed a meal of soup and fish. The man told Hans about the wonderful things which were to be found at the bottom of the sea.

On his return to the hotel where they were staying, Hans was soundly chastised by his mother – everyone had apparently been searching for him during his absence. At this point the boy declared that he would like to be a diver. He was at that time nine years old.

Hans, on another occasion, practised the art of noiseless diving with a harpoon. He was unsuccessful, harpooning only his left hand! Once he was caught by an octopus, but rescuers were at hand to free him from its tentacles. The creature measured $11\frac{1}{2}$ feet ($3\frac{1}{2}$ metres) across. Parts of it were cooked and eaten! Dolphins were also encountered – one of them when Hans was swimming in dim light. He suddenly became aware of the presence of some large creature close to him in the water, and was, at first, not surprisingly, alarmed.

When Hans was 17, his mother sent him to southern England as an exchange student, and at 18 he went to Paris for a time. On his return to Vienna he entered on a law course, with a view to taking over his father's office later. He had originally hoped to study zoology.

Hans Hass formed a group of friends whom he took on holiday expeditions to such as Dalmatia. He wrote an article for a magazine, and earned a fee of 200 marks, which enabled him to buy a camera with which to take underwater photographs. He had a watertight case built for it. Another acquisition was a pair of swimming fins, and Hass made some new harpoon heads. He wanted to teach his friends how to hunt underwater. A cutter called the *Sokel*, 26 feet (8 metres) in length, was hired at a cost of 200 dinars a day.

At Dubrovnik one of Hass's companions caught a 5 foot ($1\frac{1}{2}$ metres) long shark. Other adventures occurred when the group went to the Red Sea. Of an encounter with a shark, Hass says: "The shark was so beautiful and so elegant a fellow, and bore so little resemblance to a bloodthirsty maneater, that my one thought at this moment was how nicely he would photograph. I forgot I hadn't even a knife with me..."

A great variety of unusual fish, such as the barracuda and the porcupine fish, which puffs itself up, were found in the course of Hass's expeditions, as well as large turtles. When still in the Red Sea, Hass was once pursued by two sharks when he was 150 feet (46 metres) from the shore.

Another expedition was the *Curacao* expedition. Sea-urchins with their sharp spines posed an underwater hazard. Hass and his companions hunted for fish, which they later sold to restaur-

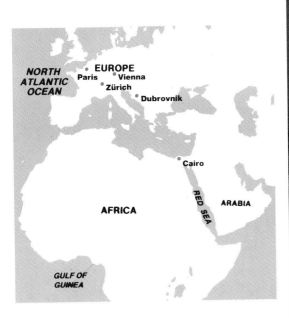

(**Above**) *One of the main dangers to divers are sharks. This Grey Reef Shark is to be found in the Red Sea. Hans Hass survived an attack by a Great White Shark.* (**Left**) *Hans Hass at work on the wreck of the Umbria.*

*The risks of those early days of underwater exploration were well rewarded by the sight of unusual sea creatures. (**Top**) The yellow butterfly fish, (**centre**) the Hawkesbill Turtle, and (**below**) the Porcupine Puffer are but three of the species found in the Red Sea.*

ants. In addition, they searched for coral to earn money for their trip home.

After marrying Lotte, the couple became well-known through their film documentaries about life under the sea which was a completely new experience for TV viewers at that time.

Trained in Pool

Lotte Hass first became associated with Hans Hass when she became his secretary. She had originally planned to study zoology. Lotte, however, was eager to accompany Hass on his expeditions, and play a more active role as a diver – a role for which Hass considered women unsuited. To bring herself up to his exacting standards she trained for half an hour every morning in an indoor swimming pool even though she was an expert diver, and already knew how an underwater camera worked. Lotte had some photographs taken by herself published in a magazine. These were seen by Hass, who was so impressed that he allowed her to join his expedition to the Red Sea. An accident forced Hass to use his secretary in a film – in a diving role.

Encounters with some of the more dangerous inhabitants of the sea were not infrequent. Sharks were a common hazard. All Lotte could do on these occasions was to remain very still until they swam off. Meetings with whale sharks were not so pleasant either, one of 24 feet (7.3 metres) swimming right under the boat. Mantas were a common sight too. They are a type of ray-fish "like a giant blanket" and have two horns.

Lotte experienced her fair share of near accidents, including losing consciousness under water, a fear always in the minds of most divers.

When crossing to Saudi Arabia on board the *El Chadra,* Hans and Lotte experienced a severe storm. So severe was it that Lotte had herself bound to the mast. The ship was forced to drop anchor, and it was later discovered that they had been close to a reef!

During a visit to Cairo, Hans Hass asked Lotte to become his wife. They were married quietly in a small town near Zurich.

MOUNTAINS, AIR
& SPACE

Sir Edmund Hillary & Tenzing Norgay

(Hillary b.1919, Tenzing 1914–1986)

Tenzing (left) and Hillary in the early stages of the Everest expedition.

The names of Hillary and Tenzing are inseparable. Their combined effort during the British Everest Expedition of 1953 (led by the then Colonel – now "Sir" John Hunt), when together they succeeded in reaching the summit of Mount Everest, led to one of the greatest achievements of mankind – as memorable in its own right as the first Moon-landing. The news of their success, arriving as it did on Coronation Day, 2nd June, 1953, gladdened the hearts of millions.

When one considers the varied career of Edmund Hillary, one cannot help wondering if his ability to adapt to ever-changing circumstances was not, eventually, to stand him in good stead when it came to facing the challenge of, for example, attempting to climb many of the highest mountains in the world, often in very adverse conditions.

Hillary was educated in Auckland, New Zealand. For many years he was an apiarist (bee-keeper). When he was nineteen he first became attracted to mountains. He had visited the Southern Alps of South Island, New Zealand. From the start, Hillary was very excited by the snow-capped peaks with the sharp black ridges

They stayed only for a quarter of an hour taking photographs. The picture of Tenzing holding his ice-axe with the tiny flags of Britain, Nepal, India and the United Nations on it is now famous. Behind their conquest lay unimaginable adventures including life and death situations – being swept towards a crevasse by an avalanche on an icy slope, being sucked into whirlpools on rafts on icy rivers, falling into crevasses and hanging upside down on a rope.

The list of Hillary's mountaineering and other expeditions is both lengthy and impressive, and includes the New Zealand Alpine Club Expedition (of which he was leader) to Barum Valley, East of Everest. Added to these, in 1955 he led the New Zealand Trans-Antarctic Expedition, and three years later he completed the overland journey to the South Pole. Later Hillary took part in jet boat expeditions up Himalayan rivers, and up the Ganges in India.

Through working frequently and closely with the Sherpas of Nepal, without whose assistance in the transportation of equipment and provisions the expeditions would have been

protruding above the white glaciers and snow which covered the mountain sides.

A Perfect Partnership

Hillary first met Sherpa Tenzing at Katmandu and he liked "the Sherpa's quiet strength and confidence" and together they formed a perfect climbing partnership. When the Everest expedition reached the final ascent it was Hillary with Tenzing who made it to the summit after several other attempts by members of their party. When they reached the summit they felt nothing but relief in the first few moments.

Hillary and Tenzing prepare for the final assault on the summit of Everest.

The famous picture of Tenzing on the summit of Everest.

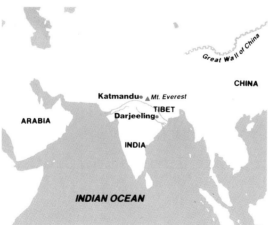

impossible, Hillary came to admire and respect these rugged, sturdy people, and eventually raised funds, through public subscription, to build a hospital for them in the Everest area. This was the first hospital for Sherpas, and a New Zealand doctor was put in charge of it.

With characteristic bravery Hillary overcame great personal tragedy and loss when, in 1975, his wife and one of his daughters were killed in a plane-crash. Another of his qualities is undoubtedly that of modesty, which has been particularly apparent in radio and television interviews.

Hillary is a member of many geographical societies, and has been the recipient of many awards, in particular a knighthood (KBE), in recognition of his many outstanding achievements. Since 1984 he has been the New Zealand High Commissioner to India. He has written books on his experiences, including *High Adventure, East of Everest* (with George Lowe), *The Crossing of Antarctica* (with Sir Vivian Fuchs) and *Nothing Venture, Nothing Win*. In addition he has travelled widely delivering lectures. His hobbies include ski-ing and camping.

Boyhood in the Mountains

Hillary and Tenzing could not have had more different backgrounds. It was their love of mountains which drew them together.

Sherpa Tenzing was born in Tibet at the foot of Mount Everest in the village of Tami in 1914. He did not know the precise day of his birth but after his triumphant conquest of Mount Everest on 29th May in 1953 he adopted that day as his birthday.

He spent his boyhood looking after his father's yaks which were taken up into the high mountain pastures. He never learned to read and write. When he was eighteen he travelled to Darjeeling and worked there as a coolie. Later he became a porter to the Himalayan Club, helping mountaineers to carry their equipment on expeditions. Good Sherpa porters are always in great demand for they have been brought up on the mountains and are knowledgeable about the area. Tenzing hoped he might be taken on as a porter for the 1933 Everest Expedition but he lacked the vital experience needed for such a venture. He cut off the pigtail worn by many

A panorama of some of the highest mountains in the world – the Himalayas.

Sherpas in the hope that it would make him look older but he was turned down. He did gain valuable experience though on other Himalayan expeditions.

During the World War II Tenzing became a guide with the Chitral Scouts, part of the Indian army. Later he became an army ski-instructor. After the war he went back to helping on numerous expeditions including climbing the east peak of Nanda Devi, until he joined the tall New Zealander, Edmund Hillary, for the assault on Everest. When they reached the top Tenzing's description is very vivid – "What we did first was what all climbers do when they reach the top of their mountain. We shook hands. But this was not enough for Everest. I waved my arms in the air, and then threw them round Hillary, and we thumped each other on the back until, even with the oxygen, we were almost breathless. Then we looked round. It was 11.30 in the morning, the sun was shining, and the sky was the deepest blue I have ever seen."

Tenzing travelled overseas a great deal after the conquest of Everest. He was famous for his infectious grin, his ability to tell a good story and he had an unconquerable spirit and a great humility which had shown itself not least in the ascent of mountains in the face of nature. He was always concerned with the welfare of other people and was a devout Buddhist. He received the George Medal from the Queen and many other honours.

Chris Bonington

(b.1934)

Christian Bonington was born in London in 1934. His parents' marriage broke up and he was brought up by his grandmother while his mother went out to work. His father was a prisoner of war for several years. Bonington led an unsettled existence for some time during which he ran away from home and school several times. It was not until he was at boarding school in Westmorland that he first encountered what was to be his greatest passion in life – mountains.

After leaving school he trained for the army at Sandhurst and served with the Royal Tank Regiment. During this time Bonington continued with his climbing and was impressed by the mountains of Wales and Scotland. On leaving the Army he became a management trainee at Unilever.

An impressive record of mountaineering achievements began in the 1960s with the Leadership/Joint-Leadership of expeditions to the Alps (for ascents of, in particular, Mont Blanc and the Eiger) and successive expeditions to the Himalayas to climb Annapurna II, Nuptse, Brammah, Changabang and, in 1985, Everest

(for the first successful ascent see Edmund Hillary page 112).

Bonington's enthusiasm for climbing and his respect for mountains is balanced by his sense of humour. This served him well in moments of drama and acute danger. When climbing Mount Freney one of his companions fell over 50 feet (15 metres) and finished dangling above Bonington's head. Even in such a moment of crisis his sense of humour did not desert him – "I've lost me 'at!" he said.

Bonington is particularly known for his photographic records of his expeditions and although he has written several books about his exploits no words can replace the atmosphere of excitement, beauty and danger of the climb.

Chris Bonington is one of the world's most experienced climbers. Not only is he a professional in every sense of the word but he has also climbed consistently tough and dangerous peaks throughout his career. These pictures show the rewards of such climbs (many of them up sheer walls of ice) — spectacular views of impressive mountain terrain.

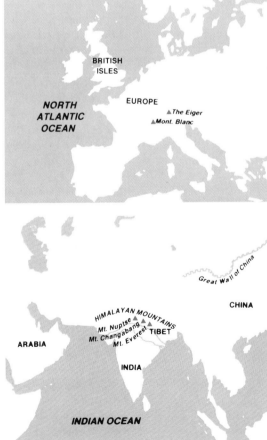

The Piccard Twins

(Auguste 1884–1962, Jean 1884–1963)

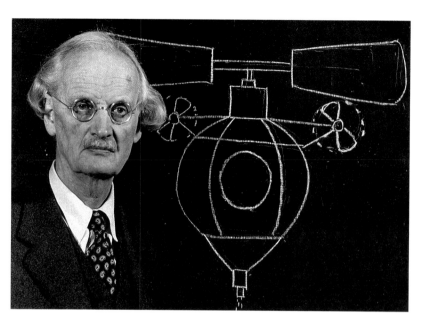

Auguste Piccard with a sketch of a "Mesoscaphe" – a diving boat he intended for use in research at depths of 1,830 metres (6,000 feet).

The Piccard twins, Auguste and Jean Felix, were born in Basle, Switzerland, where their father was a Professor of Chemistry at the University. They bore a striking likeness to each other, and it was largely the fact that Auguste was left-handed and Jean Felix right-handed that distinguished them from each other. (Both were later to become ambi-dexterous.) With a father like theirs and an uncle who was a fine engineer – he had helped to design and build turbines at Niagara Falls – it was not surprising that the twins, from an early age, developed a lively interest in science. They were always asking "Why?" At the age of ten, with their father's enthusiastic support, the twins experimented with hot-air balloons made of paper. Another great love, not surprising in a country such as Switzerland, was mountaineering.

The twins were educated at High School and at the Swiss Institute of Technology, Auguste taking his degree in Mechanical Engineering, and Jean Felix his in Chemical Engineering. They were keen balloonists, and Auguste was later to conquer the stratosphere, establish a whole new concept of ballooning, and design and develop new equipment for exploration in the upper reaches of earth's atmosphere. Auguste and Jean Felix became members of the Swiss Army Lighter-than-Air Service as auxiliaries. Jean Felix, who was to visit, and even-

tually settle, in America, planned to carry his experiments into the stratosphere where his twin had already pointed the way.

The Piccard twins found that there was a significant relationship between their experiments connected with the stratosphere, and those connected with the depths of the ocean. As boys they had been fascinated by the stories of Jules Verne.

August Piccard was keenly interested in radiation and the origins of cosmic rays which came to earth from outer space. (In 1902 the stratosphere, or vast envelope of air surrounding the earth, was discovered.) He and his twin studied methods of weather-forecasting.

In 1913 the twins made a balloon flight lasting 16 hours. They took off from Zürich and floated over France and Germany. Their aim was to measure the density and pressure of gas inside the balloon.

Separate Careers

In 1922 Auguste Piccard became a Professor at the Polytechnic Institute of Technology, at Brussels University, Belgium. In 1916 Jean Felix had gone to America, where he was to eventually settle because he felt that it was the land of the future.

Jean Felix married an American girl, Jeannette, also an identical twin. She was eager to become involved in her husband's work and underwent a course of training to enable her to become his pilot. Jean Felix continued his research work on the content of upper air at the Franklin Institute in Wilmington, Delaware. He and Jeannette made some historic balloon flights together, including a flight from Michigan to Cadiz, Ohio, crossing the dangerous Lake Erie where they were tossed about by treacherous air currents and came down, almost hitting a farm.

With the work of Auguste in Europe and Jean Felix in Delaware, weather-forecasting now became more of a science each day.

Meanwhile Auguste was anxious to find new sources of energy. He felt that the best way to study cosmic rays was to go up where they seemed to be least altered by the earth's atmosphere.

In order to try and solve some of the problems associated with his experiments on the stratosphere, Auguste Piccard decided to study the mechanical devices already successfully developed and proved, which enabled man to travel beneath the surface of the seas. Something suitable had to be invented that would be big enough to carry Auguste, his assistant and their instruments, and also provide adequate protection against unknown effects, at such heights, of cosmic radiation. It would also require to be able to protect the occupants against extremes of heat and cold, and be light enough to be lifted by a

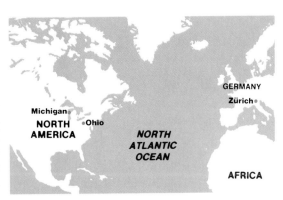

gasbag. A submarine would be too heavy. Auguste decided to devise a spherical gondola which he would suspend beneath his balloon.

Auguste Piccard, on his conquest of the stratosphere, was described as "the highest man in the world". He also helped to build the heaviest pendulum in the world, which contributed greatly to our knowledge of earthquakes.

For 40 years Auguste Piccard had been dreaming of developing his experiments in the direction of exploring the ocean at great depths. The principal dangers for divers were those incurred as a result of the enormous pressure of the water at great depths.

Auguste was convinced that the knowledge of pressures, in particular, which he had acquired through his experiments with balloons would serve him well in this sphere also.

Although another scientist, a Dr Beebe, had made many underwater discoveries using a craft called a "bathysphere", it was considered to be unsafe. Auguste Piccard wanted a vehicle which

would give maximum protection from enormous pressures at great depths, and be able to move about freely and slowly. He would try to invent an undersea "free balloon" – a bathyscaphe (in Greek, BATHOS = DEPTH, and SKAPHE = SHIP). This would enable him to roam freely at the bottom of the sea, independent of any ship above and in 1948 the first tests took place off the coast of West Africa.

(Left) Inflating the Piccard's balloons were large undertakings.
(Above) Auguste became "the highest man in the world" when he ascended into the stratosphere.

Alcock & Brown

(Alcock 1892–1919, Brown 1886–1948)

Arthur Brown (**top**) and John Alcock.

(**Right**) The twin-engined Vickers Vimy that made the first non-stop flight across the Atlantic.

When the First World War was coming to an end the possibilities for using aircraft for public transport were just beginning to be realized. It was a period of great achievement and new technological breakthroughs, and airmen such as Sir John Alcock and Sir Arthur Brown were ambitious to fly the Atlantic.

The aeroplane had for so long been seen as a "symbol of destruction" because of its use in wartime. Now prizes were being offered for air exploits and achievements, and these were changing public thinking about the aeroplane. A prize of £10,000 was offered by the London *Daily Mail* for the first non-stop flight across the Atlantic Ocean.

John Alcock, a short stocky man with ginger hair and a great love of life had flown solo before he was 20, after only two hours of instruction on the ground and in the air. He joined the Royal Naval Air Service as an instructor, and during the war underwent many daring exploits, such as the bombing of Constantinople. In 1917 his plane was forced down by anti-aircraft fire and he was taken Prisoner of War (POW) by the Turks. After the war came to an end, he joined Vickers Aircraft, manufacturers of aeroplanes, as a test pilot. He knew they were preparing to enter an aircraft for the competition and had indeed himself been formulating ideas about making just such a crossing while he was a POW.

Whereas John Alcock was full of laughter and practical jokes, Arthur Whitten Brown was a quiet serious man, shy and conventional, although he had a penetrating wit. His parents were American, but he grew up in England. He chose to fight with the British during the Great War, and trained as an engineer before becoming a pilot in the Royal Air Force.

He was shot down behind enemy lines and was a POW, in Germany, before being moved to Switzerland. He had been badly injured and although treatment in Switzerland helped him greatly he was to remain partially crippled for the rest of his life.

He too had dreamed of flying the Atlantic, but he had no idea when he visited Vickers in search of a job that the dream would become a possibility. He felt that his prospects were not bright – he was, after all, disabled – until his

interviewer asked whether Brown thought he could navigate across the Atlantic. His forceful "Yes" soon saw him being introduced to Alcock and they began preparations immediately.

By the time Alcock and Brown left Newfoundland in the Vickers Vimy aircraft they had shipped over, there had already been several attempts to cross the Atlantic. None had made it non-stop.

With much preparation behind them they were ready to set off on June 13th 1919. It was a Friday, but superstitiously they felt it was lucky even though there was a gale blowing. After all, said Alcock, the Vimy was the 13th one of its kind built, there were 13 in their party, and they had arrived on the 13th. However when they fuelled up a shock absorber broke, and Alcock

blind for three hours after take-off.

Fortunately they later ran into a spell of clearer weather. After being in the air 11 hours they flew straight into a great mass of cumulonimbus cloud, and its resulting turbulence. "The Vimy was completely out of control, plunging like a crazy horse", they later recalled. The aircraft dived steeply to straighten up only 60 feet (18 metres) above the ocean. A second storm with heavy snow and ice froze their gauges, so Brown had to climb out on the wings six times to unblock the gauges, Had he not done so the aircraft would have crashed, but his painful leg must have made each attempt a nightmare. Every time Brown went out onto the wings Alcock had to keep the plane completely steady.

At last they dropped down from 1,100 feet (335 metres) and saw land before them. The roar of the plane startled a local priest on his motorbike, so that he drove into a ditch. They were looking for a place to land, and then saw before them a patch of green. Alas it was an Irish bog, and on landing the plane was irreparably damaged, but "faces . . . unshaven and streaked with oil, their eyes red with ceaseless probing of clouds", they landed at 8.40 am. They had flown 1890 miles (3024 kilometres) non-stop, coast to coast in 15 hours 57 minutes (16 hours 27 minutes in all) at an average speed of 118 mph (189 kilometres per hour).

They were both to receive a knighthood for their courage and daring, but Alcock did not live long to enjoy his fame. On December 18th in that same year he was killed in a flying accident, when his aircraft encountered bad weather as he was making his way to the Paris Air Show. He was fatally injured.

had to suggest that maybe 14 was a luckier number after all!

Take-off

On the 14th despite initial bad weather the forecast was good and they made ready, taking aboard sandwiches, coffee, chocolates, beer and a present of a bottle of whisky. They also had their mascots, "Lucky Jim" and "Twinkletoes" – toys which they placed visibly in the small cramped plane. Someone screwed a horseshoe under Alcock's seat, and both Alcock and Brown were delighted when a lucky black cat passed under the fuselage.

Finally they were off from St John's in Newfoundland, their two Rolls Royce Eagle engines carrying them towards Europe.

They soon found out that their transmitter was useless and then they flew straight into thick fog. Shortly afterwards their exhaust broke and the deafening noise did not allow them to speak. Brown had to write notes to Alcock, but Alcock could never have both hands off the joystick at the same time, so he had to make signs to communicate with his navigator.

Worse was to come. The battery which kept their flying suits electrically warm failed. The fog at the 5000 feet (1524 metres) which they were flying remained unbroken and they flew

Amy Johnson
(1903–1941)

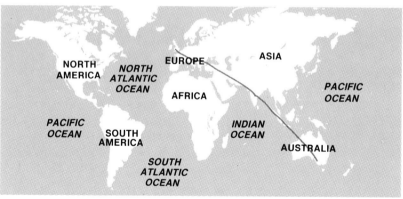

This contemporary painting by Alan Fearnley is entitled "Amy Leaves Croydon, 1930."

"Amy, Wonderful Amy," the popular song ran when Amy Johnson became the first woman to fly solo to Australia, but her path to fame was not an easy one.

She was born in Hull in 1903, the eldest of three girls and was said to be something of a rebel and was often moody. She was self-conscious because as a teenager, she had needed two false front teeth to replace ones she lost after being hit by a cricket ball.

Amy went to university and then to a teacher's training course but soon fell in love with a Swiss some years older than herself who did not reciprocate fully enough to marry her.

After trying various courses and jobs she eventually got a post as a secretary and, hoping to shock her lover into stopping her, she decided to take up flying. She had to see the bravado through and joined the London Aeroplane Club.

Her first flying lesson was not encouraging. She would never make a pilot, she was told, she had little natural aptitude. She made her first solo flight after nearly 16 hours, double the normal time for an average pilot.

However, the social side of the club and her skill at engineering helped her lose her self-consciousness and she gained her licence in 1929. She got lost on her first cross-country solo flight.

Early in 1930 she told a reporter that she was

planning a long distance flight and with help from her father and Lord Wakefield she bought a two year old Gypsy Moth which she named *Jason*.

Armed with a revolver, a mosquito net, a sun helmet, a stove, some provisions, a parachute and a fire extinguisher, she set off from Croydon in 1930. Her longest flight to date had been 147 miles (235 kilometres), and she had flown only 75 hours solo. She had a great confidence based largely on ignorance and she was setting off to beat Bert Hinkler's existing solo record of 15 days from England to Australia, some 10,000 miles (16,000 kilometres).

Damage to *Jason*

Her flight seems dogged with incidents. After landing in a desert sandstorm, she later broke a wheel strut and then went on to sheer a bolt on the replacement. She never had more than three hours sleep a day and was two days ahead of Hinkler by the time she reached Karachi. She made a forced landing at Jansi in India "wearing only a shirt, an ill-fitting pair of khaki shorts, socks and shoes, and a flying helmet . The skin on her face, arms and legs was burnt and blistered by the sun, and tears were not far from her tired eyes!"

After yet more damage was repaired she went on through monsoon rains only to land in a ditch at a football field near Rangoon. Her spare propeller was put on and the broken wing ribs repaired and the wings were covered by material from men's shirts which themselves had been made of surplus aeroplane fabrics.

She continued to meet bad weather and have crash landings on her route, somehow managing to get out of all sorts of scrapes. Aeroplanes were at that time made largely from wood and canvas and she could only carry a little fuel which meant that frequent landings had to be made.

She reached Darwin 19½ days after setting out, disappointed that she had failed to break the record but to find she was accorded a heroine's welcome. She was not able to cope with the resultant publicity and the demands made on her and she had a nervous breakdown. It would not be her last.

She was awarded £10,000 by the *Daily Mail* but soon set off on another long-distance flight,

across Siberia to China. It was winter and she had to give up after crashing near Warsaw.

She then made another record-breaking flight this time with a companion. At around the same time a nine-day flight by Jim Mollison, from Australia to England, received greater notice. This pilot was later to become her husband.

Together and separately Amy and Jim continued to break records but when they attempted a world long-distance record they crashed in America and both ended up in hospital. In America Amy became friends with another woman pilot, Amelia Earhart, the American "winged legend".

After Amy's marriage broke up she moved to Paris and though she broke further records she continued to suffer emotional strain. In 1937 she took up gliding and two years later sailing, but when war broke out she joined the women's section of Air Transport Auxiliary.

In January 1941 while on a routine flight and after more than 3000 hours in the air she died when her aircraft plunged into the sea at the mouth of the Thames. Her body was never found although her flying bag was recovered. The reports of the accident were conflicting. So too were the reasons for the accident. She might have been flying above the cloud and been blown off course; there were talks of a "secret mission", and of a passenger, but the mystery remains.

Whatever the circumstances of her death, Amy's courage, strength and luck helped her to overcome her lack of natural ability and her unhappinesses and to make her a fondly remembered pioneer in aviation history.

Dick Rutan & Jeana Yeager

(Rutan b.1938, Yeager b.1952)

On the 23rd December 1986 two adventuring pilots, Dick Rutan and Jean Yeager, touched down in the Californian desert in their fragile plane *Voyager*, having circled the world non-stop in precisely nine days and three minutes.

Voyager was the brainchild of Dick's brother Burt Rutan. In 1981 the Rutan brothers were having lunch together and made the first sketch of the *Voyager* on a table napkin! The plane that Burt designed was built so that it could carry all the fuel it needed for the non-stop round the world trip. The cockpit was tiny and cramped.

Dick Rutan had been joined by his co-pilot Jeana Yeager, a Texan girl who had met Dick while he was stunt flying in California. Before setting off on the 14th December 1986 the plane was loaded with some 1,500 US gallons (5,678 litres) of fuel. When it was fully laden the wing tips dragged on the ground. Only limited survival equipment was packed into the cockpit and they were carrying no food and water beyond what they would need for use in the air. Locked in the tiny cockpit (specially sealed until

they arrived back so as to prove they had not landed anywhere en route) Dick and Jeana saw the wing tips, weighed down by the huge load of fuel, break off as *Voyager* gathered speed along the runway. They were ordered to stop the flight because of the potential danger caused by the lack of the wing tips. Dick and Jean pleaded to be allowed to carry on and ground control gave them permission after Burt Rutan had viewed the damage from another aircraft.

The second day out saw Dick and Jeana having to make a detour over Guam in the Pacific in order to avoid a typhoon. This meant they were using up valuable extra fuel. They were, in fact, helped by strong winds which blew them onwards. From Malaysia to Africa they ran into storms. The storms were so bad over Africa that they were thrown around the cockpit. They were forced to make so many detours to avoid the worst of the storms that Dick was convinced there was not enough fuel to get them home.

As they approached the Caribbean Sea a sudden storm caused Dick to lose control of the aircraft but he managed to regain control and continued. Nearing the end of their trip engine failure caused *Voyager* to plummet 3,500 feet (1,067 metres) before Dick got on course again.

When the *Voyager* finally landed there were just 10 gallons (38 litres) of fuel left in *Voyager*'s tanks.

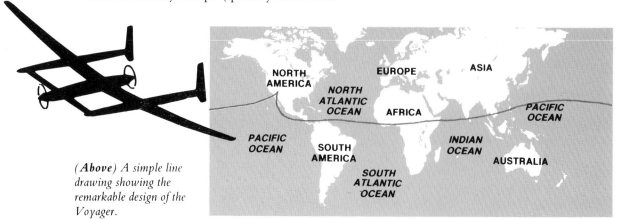

(**Above**) A simple line drawing showing the remarkable design of the Voyager.

*(**Left**) The Great Nebula in Orion.*

The age of space travel dawned in 1957 although the idea had been around since the 2nd Century when people started to enter into the realms of fantasy about such voyages. The idea became much more scientific in the late 19th Century when Konstantin Tsiolkovski, a Russian teacher, realized that any travel outside the earth's atmosphere would be powered by a rocket.

In the 1930s rocket research was carried out in Germany and after the Second World War the researchers moved to the United States and their research ended in the launching of America's first artificial satellite in 1958.

At first, only unmanned orbiters were sent up and these provided excellent maps of the entire lunar surface and the *Luna* and *Surveyor* made actual landings on the moon. However, by this time Russia had sent *Vostok 1* on an orbit of the earth carrying the cosmonaut Yuri Gagarin and less than a month later the Americans sent Alan Shepard in a short sub-orbital journey which lasted a quarter of an hour. It was just a matter of time before there would be a man on the moon.

The First Man in Space

Yuri Gagarin (1934–1968) was the first great name of travel in outer space. He was the first man to fly in outer space and captured the imagination of the world. The historic event took place on 12th April 1961 using the space craft *Vostok I* which circled the globe in 1 hour 48 minutes before returning safely to earth.

Yuri Gagarin was born in Russia in March 1934. He grew up as the youngest of three children. His parents worked on a collective farm near Gzhatsk and Yuri had a very happy childhood playing in the fruit-garden, climbing trees, racing through the forest and swimming in the river Dnieper which created in him a love of adventure.

He did well in his studies and gained a place at Saratov Industrial Technicum where he first learned to fly. He became one of the most talented and courageous fighter pilots and because of his achievements, Gagarin was selected to join a detachment of cosmonauts.

In 1961, at the age of only 27, he made his historic flight which turned him from a virtually unknown man into an international celebrity. He had proved that man could travel in outer space. Even after returning to earth he still continued to improve his skills as a pilot and cosmonaut. He helped train cosmonaut crews and he directed many subsequent space flights. Like pop idols of today he visited many countries, appeared at exhibitions and conferences and received many awards and honours. With his

bright smile and boyish features he was always popular.

Sadly, in 1968, while on a training flight he died in a tragic crash. It was ironic that he should lose his life in this way. He was buried in Red Square in Moscow, a rare honour for a Soviet citizen but a fitting one for a Hero of the Soviet Union. In his memory, a crater on the far side of the moon was named after him.

The First Woman in Space

The world of space exploration has been dominated by men since the launch of the first sputnik. The Russians were the first to break this pattern by sending Valentina Tereshkova (b.1937) into orbit on the 16th June 1963.

Valentina was a former mill worker who had been selected from those humble beginnings to become the first woman to overcome the force of gravity in the same way that the men had done before her. By doing this she broke the century-old prejudice that women had only a secondary role in the life of human society. She was not a famous pilot and after her historic flight very little has been written about her but at the time of her flight there was much excitement.

(Above) *Yuri Gagarin*
(Right) *Valentina Tereshkova*

The Moon Landing
20th July 1969

On 16th July 1969, Neil Armstrong, Edwin Aldrin and Michael Collins blasted off from Cape Canaveral in *Apollo II*. Carried aboard *Apollo* was *Eagle* the lunar module which was to drop the explorers onto the Moon.

All three men had been in space before in the Gemini program which had been part of the research needed to mount a full moon landing. Neil Armstrong had had a narrow escape in

(Above) *Alan Shephard, first American in space, standing on the Moon.* *(Left)* *Edwin Aldrin* *stands on the Moon. Reflected in his facepiece is the entire scene, including the lunar module.*

Gemini 8 when he found himself in trouble after docking with a rocket in outer space. His spacecraft started to roll from side to side and to tumble and only with skilful handling by Armstrong and his co-pilot were they able to stop the tumbling by using power bursts from their own rocket motor. They separated from the rocket successfully and returned to earth.

Aldrin had been part of the crew in the last vehicle in the Gemini series and had "walked" in space outside the capsule for over two hours.

The great difference between these explorers and those of the past was the fact that millions of people around the world were watching the whole episode live. There was great excitement and yet some fear as, if things did go wrong, there was very little chance of rescue. Arm-

strong had to steer the *Eagle* away from a huge crater before he landed and when they did eventually touch down safely all the viewers must have felt relieved. It was some half-hour later that Armstrong came down the ladder and stepped onto the Sea of Tranquility. He then spoke his now famous words "That's one small step for a man, one giant leap for mankind". Soon Aldrin had joined him. Collins remained on board to man the *Eagle* having gone "ninety per cent of the way".

The crew of the Challenger who were destined for the 25th *Shuttle flight which ended in tragedy on 28th January 1986. (**Right**).*

Robert Crippen. The space vehicle was known as *Columbia*. Two years later a new Shuttle known as *Challenger* lifted off and was commanded by Paul Weitz. After this followed a series of *Challenger* expeditions. By this time the crews were not confined to men – women began to be included on some of the flights. Sally Ride is probably among the most famous of these.

The Shuttle program has not been without its horrors. At the beginning of 1986 one of these American dreams was blown from the sky. Aboard the *Challenger* as part of a crew of seven, teacher Christa McAuliffe was to have delivered a science lesson to millions of expectant viewers. Instead those viewers watched the unthinkable happen. *Challenger* exploded in a clear blue sky only 73 seconds after leaving earth. All the crew were killed. The rocket boosters had been damaged by extreme cold.

Challenger had become something of a routine – rather like getting onto an aeroplane. The disintegration of the 25th Shuttle flight proved it was not so. It was an incident which touched people worldwide. Despite advanced technology such things can still happen to people who chance their lives in order to experience adventure and further the knowledge of mankind.

The Space Shuttle

Another stage on from the moonflights has been the development of the Space Shuttle. The cost of space travel was enormous, mainly because of the fact that a rocket can be used only once and a new one had to be built for every flight. A space vehicle capable of being used many times over was needed and eventually the Space Shuttle was developed.

It is said that the Shuttle "takes off like a rocket, flies like a space-ship and lands like a glider". It took a long time to develop the Shuttle but finally, in 1981, the first Shuttle was launched on the 12th April. This was twenty years after Yuri Gagarin's historic flight. The first pilot was John Young who had already been to the Moon in *Apollo 16*. His co-pilot was

The Earth sets over the horizon of the Moon.

ACKNOWLEDGEMENTS

Illustrations: John Charles: 6, 50, 66, 73, 84, 89.
Gerry Collins: All diagrammatic maps.

Picture credits: **T** = Top **L** = Left **R** = Right
C = Centre **B** = Bottom
Aldus Archive: **9, 10, 11, 12, 13, 14, 15, 16, 17, 22R, 24, 25, 26B, 28, 29, 31R, 35R, 36, 37, 38, 40, 41, 43, 44, 46, 48–9, 53, 61T, 67, 68, 69, 71, 72, 74, 75T, 76–7, 78, 79, 81, 88B, 90, 91, 92–3, 95, 99**; Aspect Picture Library: **122**; British Museum: **33, 67R**; Bodleian Library, Oxford/Aldus: **17T, 17C, 32C**; Chris Bonington: **116, 117**; Camera Press: **124**; Giles Chichester/Aldus: **100TL**; John Cleare Mountain Camera: **115**; ET Archive: **90T, 91B, 92T, 94T**; Mary Evans Picture Library: **96, 97, 119**; Robert Harding Picture Library: **70**; Pat Hodgson Picture Library: **21**; The Hutchison Library: **64R**; Jack Jackson: **108, 109T, 109B, 110**; Mary Kingsley, "West Africa Studies": **63**; Mansell Collection: **18T, 28T, 35, 52L, 54T, 54C, 120**; MB: **32, 86, 87**; Metropolitan Museum of Art, New York: **20**; Keith Morris: **107**; John Murray Publishers: **64, 65**; NASA: **127, 129**; National Maritime Museum: **19L, 30, 42T, 45**; National Optical Astronomy Observatories: **25**; National Portrait Gallery: **88**; Novosti Press: **126**; Popperfoto: **80, 98, 99BL, 118, 119R**; Quadrant Picture Library: **120–1**; Rex Features: **106T, 111**; John Ridgway: **104TL, 105**; Jacques Redon: **103**; Sir Alec Rose: **102**; Peter Rowlands: **106–7**; Royal Commonwealth Society: **62**; Royal Geographical Society: **57R, 60, 61, 75B, 82, 83, 112, 113, 114**; RGS/Aldus: **54B, 58, 59, 61B, 74, 75C, 83, 88T, 92–3**; RGS/Weidenfeld & Nicolson: **78T**; Victoria and Albert Museum/MB: **87**; James Weddell, "Voyage Towards the South Pole": **74**; Weidenfeld & Nicolson Ltd.: **18, 19, 22, 26T, 26–7, 33, 34, 42, 46, 51, 52R, 55, 56, 57TL, 71T, 72BR, 76, 85, 86, 87B**; ZEFA: **128**.